PATTERNS OF ETHICS

In America Today

RELIGION AND CIVILIZATION SERIES

RELIGION AND CIVILIZATION SERIES

PATTERNS OF ETHICS

In America Today

EDITED BY

F. Ernest Johnson

PROFESSOR EMERITUS OF EDUCATION, TEACHERS
COLLEGE, COLUMBIA UNIVERSITY

Published by

The INSTITUTE for RELIGIOUS and SOCIAL STUDIES. Jewish

— Theological seminary of America.

Distributed by

HARPER & BROTHERS

NEW YORK

PRINTED IN THE UNITED STATES OF AMERICA
BY THE VAIL-BALLOU PRESS, INC., BINGHAMTON, N.Y.

This book is a symposium based on lectures given at The Institute for Religious and Social Studies of The Jewish Theological Seminary of America during the winter of 1957–1958. The writers have been free to revise and expand their lectures as originally prepared. The purpose and plan of the series are explained in the Introduction.

Each chapter represents solely the individual opinions of the writer. Neither the Institute nor the editor assumes responsibility for the views expressed. The contributors were invited to address the Institute because of the special contribution each could make to general knowledge of the subject.

This is a Jacob Ziskind Memorial publication.

CONTENTS

INTRODUCTION

This book is a companion volume to *Patterns of Faith in America Today,* published by the Institute in 1957. The reader who is familiar with the latter will note at once a similarity in plan and method. Each of the writers invited to address the Institute and contribute to the volume was chosen on the basis of scholarship and special qualifications for interpreting a significant body of ethical thought and teaching in contemporary American life. In the main the ethical outlooks thus presented are those of major religious groups, but they include patterns of ethical thought and discipline that have no definitive relation to organized religion.

As in the preparation of the earlier volume, an effort was made to achieve comparability in content and treatment by focussing on problems and issues that were agreed upon as of basic importance. At the same time, each speaker was accorded latitude with respect to organization and emphasis and also to the range of subject-matter covered. One chapter, Dean Muelder's, is designedly outside the general pattern for reasons which the title makes apparent.

In organizing the material for publication a somewhat novel plan has been followed. Instead of presenting the various "systems" in the order of their relative contemporary influence as indicated by numbers of adherents, the editor, who was moderator of the course, has chosen relative antiquity as a guide to priority of presentation, so far as organized bodies of thought and teaching are concerned.

The interpreters of the several traditions were asked to discuss the nature and source of ethical sanctions and the ways in which ethical decisions are arrived at. They were asked also to give attention to specific questions in such areas as government initiative in relation to private enterprise; the moral limits of the will to national survival; religious freedom for minority groups, particularly nonreligious minorities; and family life—for example, questions concerning divorce, intermarriage, and planned parenthood.

I think it in order to point up some features of the discussion and to indicate their relevance to contemporary concerns and tensions both in religious circles and in American life and thought. Such a symposium as this is subject to the paradoxical comment that its strength is its weakness. That is to say, straightforward, individual presentations of disputed positions by those who hold strongly to them, is indispensable if there is to be any intellectual confrontation at all; yet this untrammelled witnessing to personal and group convictions always incurs the danger of overstressing distinctive views by singling out particular facets of issues on which those testifying are strongly committed with the result that the extent of agreement is obscured. This is not an unmixed evil, since a major fault of a pluralistic and more or less secularized society is "indifferentism" with respect to religious affiliation and commitment; yet it is regrettable to the extent that it hinders a common and confident commitment to ethical goals that are of equal validity and importance to the entire community. A major need of our time is to find a basis of common commitment to ethical ends that is more than a superficial and false assumption that creedal differences are not significant. If a viable definition of secularism—a much abused word—is possible, it has to do with the all too common tendency to assimilate differences in faith to differences of skin color or language as things that "don't really matter."

I think the present volume contributes importantly to clarification of this problem, which is basically a matter of finding a sufficient support in personal conviction and attachment for what is essential to the integrity of community life without disparagement of the spiritual "goods" which have a limited but powerful appeal. Only in such terms can the concept of cultural pluralism be given meaning and permanent significance.

Experience both in general education and in religious affairs has impressed me with the perennial danger that specific commitments and loyalties, and distinctive conceptions of what is essential, will be either eroded by the "acids of modernity" or exalted to so high a level that they obscure and frustrate the essential unity of concern and awareness of destiny without which society ceases to have any permanent meaning. To put it in more familiar terms, the concept of "unity in diversity" is in urgent need of clarification if cultural pluralism is not to become an empty, and even a mischievous, phrase.

Turning to more specific questions, we are all, perhaps, confused by the way in which the words "moral" and "ethical" are now equated, now distinguished, on very plausible grounds. Our writers have their own preferences, which perhaps need only to be stated, not defended. The reader, however, will do well to recognize the distinctions made as preferential rather than definitive. For example, confining the word moral to the area of consensus (*mores*) may serve a writer's purpose in quite legitimate fashion without altering the common usage which tends to equate morality and ethics. Arbitrary definitions are often necessary in the course of exposition, but in this instance one cannot overlook the fact that "ethical codes" for occupational groups are in reality derivatives from the *mores,* carrying only the freightage of moral judgment that "the traffic will bear." To say this is in no sense to detract from the importance of moral challenge in contrast to conformity; rather it is to remind ourselves that, whatever vocabulary we use, it is consensus, common societal judgment, that constitutes effectual sanctions in human affairs.

A conspicuous feature of this symposium is the difference of opinion as to the relation between ethics (or morals) and religion. It would seem useful to bear in mind as one reads that the possibility of maintaining ethical sensitiveness without any clearly defined religious faith is a simple empirical fact. What remains undemonstrated is whether or not, generation after generation, a "Puritan conscience" will sustain itself without the undergirding of something approximating a Puritan's faith. Moreover, there is danger in the course of logical argument of losing sight of the possibility that the basic relation between the spheres of religion and morality may be less a matter of sanctions than of spiritual discipline through which commitment to a way of life becomes substantial and permanent. Also, with the multiplication of ideologies and secular faiths it becomes increasingly necessary to ask not only what religion *is,* but what can *function as* religion in a given situation.

It is refreshing to read from the pen of a devout Protestant the frank statement that no solution has been found in Protestantism for the problem of authority. As a matter of fact the problem of institutional authority is always with us in both the religious and the secular sphere. The exaltation of the individual conscience, the ultimacy of whose mandate is recognized even by the most authoritarian of our churches, is evidence that a basic concern in our culture is the reconciliation of authority with liberty— the finding of a source of authority "whose service is perfect freedom."

Running through the expositions offered in this book is a theme that is acquiring central importance in the field of social ethics. I refer to the continuing concern and controversy over what is often called "situational ethics," by way of distinction from an ethics of fixed "principles." It is an issue as important as it is treacherous. Many contemporary critics of public policy-making, particularly in foreign relations, deplore the tendency to "moralistic" thinking, the essence of which is to seek, and to imagine one has found, viable answers to involved and difficult ethical questions by finding a given principle that "fits" and applying a self-evident solution of a moral dilemma. There is something spurious and exceedingly precarious about this. It leads to erroneous judgments, supported by seeming self-assurance. Yet the effort to avoid it is likewise beset by danger—the danger of reducing distinctions between right and wrong to judgments that are merely punctiliar, conditioned upon immediate circumstance and without grounding in moral principle.

In part this difficulty reflects what I think is an unfortunate confusion over what is known as "casuistry." Protestants are always distrustful of it because it looks to them like an oversimplified and convenient scheme of settling important issues which may have unusual and peculiar features, by applying ready-to-hand rules. Yet a casuistry that is really a "case" approach to ethical problems has as much to be said for it as a similar approach in law or medicine. It may even be said that the goal of a valid ethical system is the rendering of consistent and viable value judgments that are at once in line with empirical facts and in harmony with the most authentic norms that man's reason and inspired imagination have been able to construct.

It was probably inevitable that the task we set ourselves in this symposium should lead us into the much discussed and never settled issues concerning the efficacy of reason and the relation between science and values. It interests me that the spokesman for rationalism in our series should find the ultimate validation of reason in its instrumentation of a passion for excellence and should define science as "description without adjectives of value." If a passage here and there in the lectures seems to merge the categories of fact and value, thus depriving ethics of a distinctive sphere and function, I think the intention was the sound and laudable one of resisting a mischievous antiscientific mood that often finds expression in moral discourse. None of our writers would call science a "way of life"; yet none would deny the direct relevance and indispensable role of science in the enrichment of the human spirit. All, I think, would agree with Professor Harold D. Lasswell, one of the most effective participants in the activities of this Institute, that "the potential impact of the behavioral sciences is to give depth and scope to the interaction of norms and knowledge and to supplement the formulation of norms with the application of procedures capable of narrowing the gap between aspiration and actuality."

THE EDITOR

May, 1959

I

ETHICS OF JUDAISM

BY

MAX J. ROUTTENBERG

*Rabbi, Temple B'nai Sholom
of Rockville Centre*

When President Roosevelt was asked, during the dark days of World War II, why were we waging this war, he replied: "In defense of one verse in Genesis, 'God created man in His own image.'" In this reply, Roosevelt not only formulated the essence of democracy, but expounded the basic ethical tradition of both Judaism and Christianity—the sacredness of each individual human being. Man, formed in God's image and possessed of the divine spirit which was breathed into him, is the crown and glory of God's creation. In Judaism it is this concept of man, created in God's image, which forms the foundation of Jewish ethics.

It will be instructive to see how this concept was developed in normative Jewish teaching. On the basis of this verse in Genesis, the Rabbis of the Talmud make the following observations:

Man was created through Adam, a single human being, in order to teach that whoever destroys a single human life is regarded as though he destroyed an entire world, and he who saves a single human life is as though he saved an entire world. The human race began with a single individual for the sake of peace among all men, so that no man might say, "My ancestor is greater than yours." Moreover, the creation of humanity through one ancestor proclaims the greatness of the Holy One, blessed be He. For man strikes off many coins with a single mould and they are all identical. But the Holy One, blessed be He,

7

stamps each man in the mould of Adam, and yet no one is identical with his fellow. The creation of Adam teaches that each human being is obligated to say, "For my sake was the world created" (Mishna, Sanhedrin, Chapter 4).

In this teaching the Rabbis used the Biblical account of creation to teach the innate dignity and equality of every man and the sacredness of human life. From this, it follows clearly what man's duty is to his fellow man—this duty is succinctly embodied in the command as stated in the nineteenth chapter of Leviticus, "Thou shalt love thy neighbor as thyself, I am the Lord." And to emphasize that "thy neighbor" is not to be understood in an exclusive sense, we have in the same chapter (v. 34) the injunction concerning the stranger "and thou shalt love him as thyself." Rabbi Akiba regarded this commandment to love one's fellow man as the quintessence of the Torah: his illustrious predecessor Hillel gave it a different formulation when he was asked for the essence of Jewish teaching—that which is hateful unto thee do not do unto thy neighbor.

From this central doctrine of man's sacredness, flow all the specific teachings concerning man's inalienable rights: he is entitled to freedom so that he may fulfil his divine potentialities and every form of slavery is a violation of the sacredness of his personality; he is entitled to justice so that his unique goals and purposes as an individual may not be prevented or thwarted; he is entitled to peace and security so that he may live without danger to his life and without any diminution of his rights to happiness and well-being. From this doctrine flow not only his rights and privileges but also his duties and his responsibilities, which we shall discuss later.

In Judaism there has grown up a threefold technique for transmitting the ethical doctrines as formulated by its authoritative teachers. First was the technique of preaching. This was the method of Moses and all the prophets who followed him. Through exhortation, through homily, through parable, now chiding, now pleading, now threatening, the Jewish moralists through the ages brought the doctrines of a good life with force and eloquence to the attention of the people. "What doth the Lord require of thee, but to do justly, to love mercy and walk humbly with thy God." "Have we not all one Father? Hath not one God created us? Why do we deal treacherously, every man against his brother?" "And now, O Israel, what doth the Lord thy God ask of thee, but to serve the Lord thy God, to walk in all His ways and to love Him, and to serve the Lord thy God with all thy heart and all thy soul." These were the sermons, the preachments, wherewith the great preachers of Israel exhorted the people to follow the ethical life as commanded by God. All these teachings may be subsumed under the one general principle of ethical monotheism. God is a God of love, of justice, of righteousness, and if He created us then He created us for the specific role of enacting His will and His purpose on this earth. That purpose is not exhausted by the command to love our neighbor. God created the entire universe and all that is in it, and our love must embrace all of His creation. As the late Rabbi Kook put it: "When we know and love God we cannot help but feel the love of the universe, the love of all the worlds, of all creatures, and their realms of life and being." Here is a structure of universal morality emerging from the conception of the oneness and ethical character of a God Who is the creator of the universe.

Judaism, however, did not confine itself merely to the enunciation of general moral principles, through preachment and exhortation; it developed a unique system of education which was designed to transmit the principles of ethical monotheism to every man. The obligation to know and understand the moral teachings of Judaism is a prime duty of every Jew, not just the rabbi, the scholar, or the teachers. The ancient Rabbis had a favorite saying: "The ignorant man cannot be devout." The life of reason they regarded as necessary so that man would reveal the Divinity that was in him. For man's kinship with God is no better asserted or His nature more effectively imitated than in the search for truth. The Torah is not just to be received or believed in, it is to be studied. Thus, as early as the first century of this era, Jews had developed a system of elementary and secondary education. For the adults there were study groups on week-day evenings and Sabbath afternoons, when there was instruction in Bible and Talmud, as well as the study of popular ethical treatises, such as "The Ethics of the Fathers," "The Duties of the Heart," and the "Paths of the Righteous."

Combined with study as an instrument of education, Judaism developed another educational technique for transmitting the moral law. This was the system of symbols and ceremonies which entered the life of the individual in vivid and dramatic fashion. The Sabbath, for example, expressed the universal sanctity of all life as an act of the Creator. The Sabbath symbolized the divine glory manifest in all existence, as well as man's duty to treat all of creation with the utmost reverence and respect. He was thus required to avoid any manner of work which would disturb the peace of the world, of other human beings, of animals, of plants, and even of inanimate objects. It was for this reason that the Rabbis extolled the Sabbath as the institution which embodied all the essential teachings of Judaism, a symbol of the perfect world toward which all of mankind was striving. On the New Year and the Day of Atonement man was summoned to introspection and repentance, to a critical evaluation of his life so that he could reach out for wider moral horizons. Every Jew was required to affix a *Mezuzah* on the doorposts of his home and his place of business, for in the *Mezuzah* are contained Scriptural passages which declare the oneness and universal presence of God, thereby bringing to his consciousness almost every moment of the day an awareness of God and the imperative to act according to His will. These same passages appear in the phylacteries which the Jew wears at morning week-day prayers, on his head and on his arm, thereby consecrating both thought and deed to the service of God.

But that was not yet sufficient to ensure the practice of the moral life. Men believe in God, act out the symbols and the ceremonies as prescribed, yet deal treacherously with their fellow men. And so Judaism created a third and climactic technique for the transmission of ethical doctrine, a system of law which would lead man from general principles to the concrete imperatives derived therefrom. It is not our purpose in this paper to defend this seemingly incongruous appearance of a legal code in the realm of the moral life. But a word ought to be said in explanation of this unique Jewish creation, a system of jurisprudence as an aid to an ethical pattern of life. Law is present in Judaism because, first and foremost, it is part of the Torah tradition. But it remains a permanent element in Jewish life because of historic Jewish insistence that our ethical ideals must be put to work; they must be translated into habits and disciplines, they must be made incarnate in institutions, ceremonials, and in law. Otherwise these principles would be left as empty vessels, without urgency and without content. Impelled by a vigorous ethical idealism, Judaism has been determined to put this idealism to work in the everyday life of its adherents.

Judaism teaches that man is made in the image of God. Therefore, the law is that the stranger may not be oppressed, the wages of a hired servantman not be withheld; the slave girl shall be protected against abuse by her master; no man shall bear the penalty of another's guilt; a creditor may not enter the house of the debtor to claim payment; the slaying of a slave is as much murder as the killing of a free man; and when the bondman goes free he shall be compensated by severance pay.

Judaism teaches that human life is a divine gift and it is therefore sacred. The law, then, requires that one must guard and protect one's own life. Suicide is a gross moral wrong, for it represents the rejection of what God has given. A person is forbidden to place his life in jeopardy without due cause. Man's first obligation is to himself, therefore his life has priority over the lives of others. Self-defense, Jewish law declares, is a moral duty even when it includes taking the life of an assailant. On the other hand, if a tyrannical power, as an act of punishment, demands of a group that one of their number be selected for death, they are forbidden to do so even if their refusal dooms all of them to death. A man has no right to save his life by bringing death to his neighbor, except in defense against attack. The sanctity of life includes all of God's creatures, for anything that God has created has worth and significance. Jewish law was very emphatic in its opposition to the sport of hunting. While it permitted the eating of meat, it sought to protect animal life against abuse; thus, it outlawed the pagan practice of cutting organs from a living animal, and adopted a procedure that would inflict a minimum amount of pain in slaughtering animals for food.

Judaism teaches that all men are equal before God, they are all brothers owing each other fraternal solicitude. The law then states: let a tithe be taken for the needy; the poor may lawfully claim for themselves the corners of the fields, the gleanings, and anything overlooked in the harvesting. Anyone who requires it, may enter a field to eat, though he may not carry anything away. Hence also the accepting of interest is prohibited, nor may a millstone or garment be taken as security.

Jewish law grew out of the Biblical legislation and flowered in the days of the Mishna and the Talmud. The Rabbinic legislators displayed the same passion for love of God and love of man, for justice and mercy, as did the prophets. Applying the doctrine of ethical monotheism to this situation, they expanded the horizon of personal and social ethics. They challenged the practice of capital punishment and virtually abolished it in their courts. They virtually legislated Hebrew slavery out of existence. They guaranteed the right of the working man to strike. They established a legal presumption in favor of labor in disputes between workers and their employers. They instituted universal compulsory education. They protected zealously the rights of women and improved their status.

This approach to the ethical life, summoning man to perform the will of God, through preachment, education, and legislation, is based on certain presuppositions. It is based, in the first instance, on the thesis that life is good and not evil. "And God saw everything that He had made and behold it was very good." Therefore, a man must treasure life and not despise it, have faith in it and never despair of its possibilities. Life is good and man can find it such, provided that he chooses to live it properly. In the second instance, Jewish ethics is based on the belief that man, created in the image of God, is good and not evil, and that he displays in his life the powers ascribed to the Divinity: the ability to think and create, the awareness of the good and the beautiful, the capacity for love and compassion, and the freedom of will to choose the good life, as it is written: "See, I have set before thee this day life and good, and death and evil, in that I command thee this day, to love the Lord thy God, to walk in His ways, and to keep His commandments and His statutes and His ordinances . . . therefore choose life, that thou mayest live, thou and thy seed."

What about evil in the world? What about man's sinfulness? Surely any realistic system of ethics must reckon with these obvious conditions of human existence. And if Judaism is anything, it is certainly practical, realistic, and is not given to blind optimism about the nature of the world and the nature of man. There is no single response in Judaism to the problem of evil and disorder and suffering in the good world that the God of goodness created. It offers many answers framed by all its great teachers who wrestled with the problem. These answers come to us in moral terms and in metaphysical terms; perhaps the closest to a typically Jewish view of evil is that it is inscrutable and the answer is known to God alone. This is the note on which the Book of Job ends. This is the meaning of the Rabbinic saying: "It is not in our power to explain either the tranquillity of the wicked or the sufferings of the righteous." Here again Judaism runs true to character and its primary concern is not with theories about evil but with man's behavior in the face of evil which he encounters. Judaism expects a man, no matter what else he may think about evil, to recognize it as something that must be fought and to go out and fight it. Judaism rejects the dogmatic pessimism of those religions which teach that this world is irremediably evil: that man should practice uncompromising non-resistance, that there is no possibility of happiness in this world and the effort to improve it means to sink deeper and deeper into a morass of involvement and attachment; that the wise man seeks a way of escape from it, not ways of ameliorating it.

Judaism does not accept the doctrine of non-resistance. It demands action from its adherents. It teaches that there is evil in society and that it is man's duty to overcome it—if need be by force, though force is not the only way in which evil can be overcome. The only refuge from the cruel wrongs of the world is the effort to set them aright. There is in Judaism no ethics of resignation or withdrawal from the world. Judaism recognizes that there are certain evils which cannot be eradicated, certain uncorrectable evils which are the lot of all men. Man cannot do away with death or the accidental tragedies of life. They are inherent in the very structure of human existence. But Judaism expects man to endure these with dignity and courage, mitigating this bitterness and hurt with a sublime faith in God's essential goodness, utilizing them, because he must, for the purification and refinement of his soul.

Where man can do something to mitigate evil, it is his moral duty to do it. He can reduce the incidence of disease and accidents. He can lessen pain and physical suffering. He can put an end to social evils. He can eradicate poverty and war, which are, perhaps, the chief sources of human misery and suffering. If one lives in a community of poverty, political corruption, crime, and the perversion of justice, Judaism insists that one must not accept them as inevitable, or say "It is God's problem and in His own good time He will set things aright, while I go look after the salvation of my soul." Over and over again the Bible admonishes! "And thou shalt eradicate the evil from your midst." The prophet Isaiah cries out: "Seek justice, combat oppression, defend the fatherless, plead for the widow." Tyrants and oppressors must be fought. Insurrection and revolution against tyranny are, under certain conditions, not only justified but mandatory. Judaism teaches that it is not enough to love what is good—one must at the same time hate evil. As the Psalmist expressed it: "Ye that love God, hate evil." If one sees his neighbor attacked and in danger, he must not stand idly by the blood of his neighbor, he must run to his assistance, even if it means endangering his own life. One dare not say at such a moment, "I do not believe in violence, I believe in non-resistance." Judaism does not hold that we can solve the problem of evil by turning the other cheek to the smiter. In the Jewish view, this is an unnatural principle, as it urges acquiescence in injustice; and injustice is never to be acquiesced in, no matter whom or where it strikes, not even when it strikes me.

Alongside the duty of resistance, Judaism also teaches the duty of forbearance. The Rabbis say: A man should always be willing to forgive an insult or an injury done to him. It is, at times, an act of great nobility of spirit to be patient with personal abuse, insult, and wrong. Certainly no one should stoop to personal vengeance. In Proverbs we read: "Say not I will pay back the evil that was done to me" (Pr. 20:22). The Book of Ecclesiasticus teaches: "He that taketh vengeance shall find vengeance from the Lord, and God will keep his sins in remembrance. Forgive thy neighbor the hurt that he has done unto thee, so shall thy sins also be forgiven when thou prayest" (Eccles. 28:1–2). It is one thing, however, to be forbearing and forgiving; it is another to submit to evil as a matter of principle, to practice non-resistance to evil as a way of life.

Judaism was probably the first among the religions of mankind to project the vision of universal peace, when nations would beat their swords into plowshares and men would learn war no more. But until such an age is ushered in, Judaism does not deny nations the right of self-defense. War in self-defense is a dreadful but inescapable necessity, and citizens must take up arms to protect their country or their faith against aggressors who would destroy them. The principle of self-defense which applies to individuals: "If one comes to kill you, kill him first," applies to nations as well. The religious teachers of Israel, however, never extolled war as a national career, never regarded it a noble pursuit, but sought to humanize it as much as possible and to mitigate its horrors. Judaism hated war and the shedding of blood. "If one sheds blood it is accounted to him as though he diminished the image of God"

(Gen. 9:6). King David was denied the privilege of building the Temple because his hands had spilled much blood. And yet the Jews fought when necessary, against the armies of Antiochus, against the legions of Rome, as a matter of national survival. Judaism taught that the good society is possible, but it will not come through inaction, abdication, or despair; it will come only through resistance to evil and cooperation with the forces of good in the world.

What about the evil in man? What about his sinful nature? Highly as Judaism appraises man, it has no illusions about him. It knows full well that his character includes a great measure of depravity, that "his wickedness is great in the earth, and that every imagination of the thoughts of his heart is only evil continually," that his "heart is deceitful above all things and exceedingly weak" and that sin is ever at his door and unto it is his desire. The Rabbis see man as possessing two impulses—the *Yezer Tob* (the good impulse) and the *Yezer Ra* (the evil impulse). So God created him. Both are necessary to his nature; his egoism and his altruism are the vital tools which man needs to fulfil his vocation in the world. Man's evil impulse, his aggressive egoism, despite the mischief that it causes, is not an evil thing in itself. It must have a positive role to play in man's life or a good God would not have called it into being. Indeed, man is indebted to this evil impulse for many of the indispensable elements of his existence. When God looked upon the handiwork He had fashioned and proclaimed it as "very good," He must have included the evil impulse. So taught Rabbi Nahman ben Samuel who went on to say: "Is then the evil impulse very good? Indeed it is, for without it a person would not build a house or marry or beget children, or engage in a trade, as it is written: 'then I saw all labor and every skillful work, that it prevails through the rivalry of one against his neighbor'" (Eccles. 4:4). The drives to egoism and altruism are the raw materials of human conduct which must be properly balanced and integrated into man's character. It would have saved man a great deal of trouble, no doubt, if God had simply poured into our natures the impulse to do the good and right thing in every situation. But then we would have lost one of our most important attributes, our freedom as moral agents. For without the ability to sin and to commit error, we would not be free human beings. But by the same token, man has the power to resist sin and to overcome error, since he is the master of his own decisions. The verse in Scripture which says that sin crouches at every door, ends with the assurance: "Yet mayest thou rule over it."

Since sin is resistible, it is man's duty to resist it with all the vigor at his command. The defenses against sin which Jewish tradition has erected are numerous and mighty—prayer, the study of the Torah, absorption in good works, the companionship of the wise and the upright, and the exercise of will power. And if, nevertheless, man falls into sin, he may repent and be forgiven. The initiative, however, must come from man, not from God. God's love will meet man half-way, as Yehuda Halevi expressed it: "When I go forth to seek Thee, I find Thee seeking me." Redemption from sin begins with self-redemption and a man's anxiety for a sin committed may properly end there.

We have tried to make clear the basic doctrines which constitute the pattern of Jewish Ethics. They are subsumed under the general principle of the responsibility of man, created in God's image, to do the will of God by performing the Mizvot, the commandments of the Torah. This responsibility, in turn, is predicated on the belief that man is a free moral agent, free to choose between the conflicting impulses of his nature, between alternative courses of action, the road he desires to follow. God does not decree that a man should be good or evil. This is the point of a statement by Rabbi Hanina ben Pappa, a third century Palestinian teacher who declared: "Before a human being is conceived in his mother's womb, God has already ordained concerning him whether he shall be strong or weak, intelligent or dull, rich or poor. But whether he shall be righteous or wicked is not ordained. Not even God can determine this since it has been taught, 'all things are in Heaven's hands except man's reverence for Heaven.'"

The tradition, of course, recognizes and deals with the problem of the natural limitations of man's freedom. Since we are housed in bodies we are subject to the conditions of all things corporeal. We cannot, no matter how we may desire it, be in two places at once, or live at another time than that in which we find ourselves. We may be limited further by deficiencies in our physical or mental equipment, by conditions imposed by birth, or by large-scale social forces beyond our power to control. But within these limitations, there are open spaces in which man's freedom can operate and Judaism urges man to act as if these boundaries did not exist at all as far as his moral initiative is concerned. It is man's duty to develop his freedom, just as it is his duty to develop his reason, though that, too, has its limitations.

This is a crucial issue for our discussion. We say, "responsible decision-making lies at the root of individual and social morality." We had better understand how free man is to make responsible decisions in human affairs. How can man exercise any choice or moral initiative whatsoever, when his whole way of life is preconditioned by the society into which he is born, by its economic, social, political, and legal mores? Within the context of social repressions and traditions, is it possible for the individual to be sufficiently autonomous to master his own moral career, and to be responsible for it? I think we will find that the best thought of our day is turning away from the concept of social and cultural determinism to a view which regards man as able to fashion his own private world within the larger social framework which in itself is subject to redirection by man himself. Dr. Lawrence K. Frank has said:

We can today, I believe, offer a new and fruitful conception of culture and the individual, viewing the individual as no longer a helpless social atom, subject to the operation of vast social forces, nor as a passive member of a culture submitting to the coercion of traditions. Rather we can see the individual as the dynamic agent who, with increasing recognition of his role and place in the social order, of his inescapable but potentially creative participation in culture, can make choices, can set goals that will increasingly alter the social order and redirect the culture.[1]

[1] L. K. Frank, *Cultural Determinism and Free Will,* Hebrew Union College-Jewish Institute of Religion, Cincinnati, 1951, p. 26.

Man must work within definite limitations of environment and heredity. Knowing this should fill us with understanding and sympathy for wrongdoers. But these limitations are not ironclad, absolute, or unalterable. While man is not all-powerful, he is not powerless either. He is not a mere tool. He has resources of power within himself to accomplish very much. Man cannot escape his responsibility by unloading on God or on fate, all the evil of the world. Individuals often appear to fail, even when they choose wisely and morally. Good men have suppressed frustration and defeat, but actually there is no real failure in the pursuit of any noble objective. There is heartache and sorrow, but the grandeur of the individual's life is never dimmed by defeat, nor is his cause, if it is right, permanently denied. This is the basic postulate of the spiritual and ethical life of man as Judaism has propounded it.

It should be fairly obvious from our discussion that Judaism places upon its adherents the responsibility for fashioning their individual lives and the society in which they find themselves. It offers no easy road to salvation. It does not forsake them completely and leave them to their own devices, to exercise their judgment without guidance. The great teachers, the prophets, the rabbis have drawn up a blueprint of the good life to serve as a guide and a resource for decision-making. But these architects of the tradition lived in an age other than ours when such ideologies as democracy, totalitarianism, capitalism, socialism, and communism had not yet been conceived, and when our particular social dilemmas did not exist—at least not in their present form. And so on the crucial moral issues of our day, it is not possible to give a specific and detailed answer as to where Judaism stands. However, the Tradition is so clear in its basic social outlook that we can draw our deductions with respect to contemporary problems with a great measure of confidence. It is interesting to note that the major rabbinical bodies of this country, divided though they are by many theological and ritualistic differences, in their pronouncements on the various social issues of the day coincide in their program of action. Thus, they all agree, in the first instance, that it is the function of religion not merely to give solace to the individual in a world of travail and sorrow, but also and primarily to embody in human society those ethical ideals and spiritual values which are evidence of God's sovereignty; and, in the second instance, that the discussion of social and economic justice and the evaluation of movements to abolish war, poverty, exploitation, and other social evils are not only legitimate but necessary concerns of the Synagogue, and that teachers of religion, if they are to be true to their calling, must give voice, in unequivocal terms, to those ethical values which are relevant to man's organized living. They must, without fear or hesitation, apply these ideals as criteria of judgment upon the social order.

The modern rabbinate, on the basis of its understanding of the traditional pattern of social ethics, takes its stand on all the vital issues of our day. It calls for the fullest democracy in our economic life, in which private profit must be subordinated to public welfare. It recognizes the need of governmental action to plan and effect a balanced economy that shall insure to every human being an equal claim to those economic goods and services that are indispensable to his life and health, and to protect all against economic catastrophe. It recognizes the dangers that inhere in concentrating power in a central governmental authority which must, of necessity, curtail some of the personal liberties of individuals, but also the even greater danger in leaving to the individual himself or to private enterprise the determination of what constitutes an equitable distribution of the world's goods. Religion cannot depend completely on achieving its ethical goals, on preaching the duty we owe to love one another. For even where love exists, there is still the need of intelligent action and man requires guidance as to what he must do in behalf of those he loves. Furthermore, we must reckon with the fact that we have not only love for others, but also love for ourselves, and all too often the claims of our neighbor are made to yield before the claims of self-love. In this crucial area of human needs and happiness, it is too dangerous to leave man to struggle alone between these two loves and assume that he will always choose altruistically. It becomes, then, the duty of the government to help men make the proper choices by preventing all forms of exploitation of the weak by the strong.

Of course, religion is still involved in a dilemma when it is faced with the problem of endorsing certain specific economic measures or programs of social legislation. No social order, by its very nature, can be depended on to fulfil completely the mission charged to it. No social order is perfect, it is only perfectible. In giving its backing to a particular economic measure, religion would thereby be associating itself with a partial good, to which it can give only partial approval. But we cannot avoid this dilemma. For life moves forward by embracing partial goods. The refusal to act because we are unwilling to be involved in a choice of relative values is to adopt a policy of perfectionism which will rob life of all direction and guidance and invite not a greater good but a greater evil. Religion must, therefore, be ready to support specific programs of social action, without, however, identifying itself with those programs. Its support must always be qualified and relative.

Even as Judaism claims the right of maximum personal liberty for the individual, so does it demand for all groups of men united in voluntary association the right to the classic liberties of America, freedom of speech, of press, of conscience, and of assembly. These groups may be minorities of race, color, religion, politics, or cultural outlook. Though part of a larger social context to which they owe loyalty and whose welfare embraces them, that they are communities with distinctive unique cultural characteristics, which they must feel free to express in life. It is the very business of society to encourage minorities in their uniqueness, for by projecting a way of life other than the one dominant in this environment, they carry the seeds of a new growth for society. An existent pattern of society must not be regarded as a final achievement that is beyond criticism. Minorities, like individuals, fulfil themselves best not when they conform to the majority but when they find the distinctive note in their culture and do not abandon it.

This, too, is not without its dangers, for such liberties can be, and are, abused by minority groups who take advantage of them to impose on others restrictions of the very liberties they demand for themselves. Unrestricted and uncurtailed freedom for minorities may well result in the ultimate tyranny over the majority by a minority. Here again we are faced with the dilemma of the lesser evil: allowing unlimited freedom which may be abused, or regulating freedom to the hurt of full expression of group aspirations. In its pronouncement on this subject, the Rabbinical Assembly of America, through its Social Justice Commission, made the following statement:

While realizing the possibilities of abusing any form of legislation which would restrict the individual's expression of opinion, we nevertheless regard some limitation as less dangerous to the peace and liberty of the people than our present practice. We therefore commend the enactment of legislation which, while permitting freedom of legitimate public criticism, shall effectively curb libelous and incendiary propaganda that endangers the security and peace of law-abiding racial and religious groups in our population.[2]

In the matter of national survival, the Jewish tradition speaks clearly and unambiguously. Historically considered, Judaism has renounced military aggression and striven for peace. As teachers of Judaism, therefore, we disavow war as an instrument of national policy. We face the sad fact that mankind has failed to achieve the establishment of a just and cooperative social order that applies peaceable procedures to the resolution of conflicting national interests. Until this goal has been achieved, no nation and no religion can wash its hands of moral responsibility for war, even though in a particular conflict it may be the victim rather than the perpetrator of the offense. At the same time, we recognize that the distinction between victim and perpetrator is ethically valid and that so long as some nations do resort arbitrarily to war as an instrument of national policy, the right of others to defend themselves against this aggression cannot be justly denied. To fail to resist military aggression serves only to encourage irresponsible recourse to war and to perpetuate the sin of mankind in not

---

[2] Rabbinical Assembly Proceedings, 1941–1944, p. 47.

establishing a just and cooperative international order. As Americans we desire the government of the United States to take the lead in establishing such an order as a prerequisite to a peaceful world. The strength, the wealth, and the influence of this country impose upon us the obligation to take the lead in maintaining the processes of peaceful cooperation among the nations of the world. But it is in keeping with our best ethical insights, that we make it clear that while, on the one hand, our hope for the future is bound up with the hope of universal disarmament, with an international society banded in brotherhood, united in the law of God for justice and freedom, we shall not, on the other hand, submit passively in nonresistance to the threat of annihilation by a foreign power which would destroy our national existence.

We turn now to the ethic of marriage and divorce as it developed in the Jewish tradition. We are dealing here with an area of life which, in modern times, has been responsible for so much hypocrisy, heartache, and human misery that we need the best insights and highest wisdom to deal effectively with this most universal and most intimate of all human experiences.

Let us begin by restating the basic ethical teaching of Judaism, that since man is created in the image of God, no element of his nature is inherently evil or sinful. The body and the desires of the flesh are not evil as such, they are instruments which, when wisely used, serve man's highest purpose, the fulfilment of God's will. Marriage, then, is regarded not as a concession to the weakness of the human flesh, but as a religious obligation. Celibacy was frowned upon and we find in the Talmudic literature a record of only one celibate Rabbi, Simon ben Azzi, who apologized by stating, "I am in love with the Torah." Marriage, in Judaism, fulfils two purposes. The first is the procreation of children, in fulfilment of the command, "Be fruitful and multiply." Jewish law defines this commandment with characteristic precision. The obligation is fulfilled when two children are born. There is a dispute, however, between the two great schools of Shammai and Hillel on the question whether two male children are required, as

Shammai insists, or whether the obligation is fulfilled by having one boy and one girl, as maintained by Hillel. (Jewish law follows the decisions of Hillel.)

The second purpose of marriage is companionship. God's motive in creating Eve as a helpmeet for Adam is stated to be: "It is not good for man to dwell alone; I will make a helpmeet for him." Since she was created for him while he was yet in the Garden of Eden, before procreation was contemplated, the purpose was primarily companionship. Such companionship, involving sexual relationship, was always regarded in Judaism as a legitimate end in itself. Jewish law recommends that old and sterile persons should marry, even when there is no possibility of having children. The normative view in Judaism is that sexual relations between husband and wife are a perfectly legitimate form of pleasure which justifies itself even without the goal of procreation of children. It even permits various irregular forms of sexual play between man and wife, though it cautions against the danger of this becoming habitual and exclusive.

The true purposes of marriage, procreation of children and companionship, serve as the basis for the Rabbinic view on birth control and family limitation. On the one hand, the Rabbis frowned upon those who sought to avoid the responsibilities involved in the rearing of children for the sake of advancing their own pleasure and comfort and they insisted upon the fulfilment of the God-given duty to perpetuate the human race. On the other hand, they recognized that there were occasions and circumstances where the practice of birth control was socially desirable.

The passage in the Talmud which deals with the problem of family limitation reads as follows: "Three types of women may (the Hebrew term can also be interpreted as must) use a contraceptive in their marital intercourse, a minor (between eleven and twelve years of age), because otherwise she might become pregnant and die; a pregnant woman, lest she harm her foetus; and a nursing mother, lest she might be forced to wean her child prematurely and cause its death." There is controversy among post-Talmudic authorities as to whether these three categories of women may or must practice contraception, and whether only these three may while others may not. In any case, it is clear that there is a strong precedent for family limitation under conditions which affect the life and welfare of human beings. Rabbinic law also permitted women to avoid pregnancy where they already had borne children who were immoral or degenerate and were afraid to bring similar children into the world. It was permitted a woman to sterilize herself permanently if she could not bear the extreme pain of child bearing. From all this, it is evident that Rabbinic Judaism regarded birth control as permissible, even obligatory, in cases where the mother's life or health was involved or where she was exposed to extraordinary pain, or where the health of a child, born or unborn, would be endangered by her pregnancy. In modern Judaism there is a strong tendency to extend the conditions and circumstances cited by the tradition which permit conscious family limitation. While unequivocally reaffirming the obligation to perpetuate the human race through the medium of marriage as a basic goal, it recognizes at the same time that planned parenthood is a basic necessity of modern life, in view of the whole complex of social, economic, hygienic, and moral factors surrounding the present-day family. We ought to mention one other great virtue in planned parenthood which appeals to the Jewish view of marriage, namely, that it enables young people to marry early. Our economic system often requires that both husband and wife work, at least during the first few years of marriage. The Rabbis were quite realistic about the dangers of late marriages and did not pretend that most men and women would abstain from sexual experience until their later years. They said: "He who reaches the age of twenty and does not marry, spends all his days in sin—or at least in the thought of sin."

With regard to divorce, Jewish law is very liberal, offering release when a marriage has become intolerable. We are confronted here with a curious paradox—that while the law is lenient with regard to divorce, the attitude in Jewish life has been very severe and every effort was exerted to maintain the permanence of the marriage bond. All the resources of the tradition were brought to bear on husband and wife to make them appreciate the sacredness of their union. "He who divorces his first wife, even the altar of the Temple sheds tears for him," the Rabbis declared.

When it became evident, however, that the marriage had failed beyond repair, Judaism recognized that the union had lost its sanctity, for love and mutual respect are the basic conditions for God's presence in the home. When these no longer obtain, then it is as though husband and wife are no longer joined together by God.

In Jewish law divorce is regarded as a frank recognition that the marriage has been unsuccessful. The grounds of divorce, therefore, go beyond adultery. The fact that both partners to the marriage recognize that they cannot live happily, or at least tolerably well, together constitutes the strongest grounds for the issuing of a writ of divorcement. Rabbinic law lists many possible causes for divorce, including incompatibility, undesirable personal habits, or even occupation. There are others which seem quite trivial and superficial—the husband's charge that the wife burns the meals she serves, or the wife's charge that the husband suffers from bad breath, or from an unpleasant disease. One of the most frequently quoted is Rabbi Akiba's statement that a man may divorce his wife "if he finds another woman more attractive." We must set this statement against the experience of his own marriage which the Talmud describes as one of the great romantic love idylls of history. To him it seemed inconceivable that any man could love another woman more than his own wife, and when such a situation obtained the man's marriage was defiled and should be dissolved. In a word, the Rabbis were saying that when the community of spirit between husband and wife ceased to exist, the very essence of this marriage has been destroyed and it should be legally put to an end.

In the traditional Jewish community, powerful religious and social factors were at work to preserve the sense of sanctity of marriage and the conviction that marriage was a permanent status. As a result, divorce was rarely resorted to, and then only after all efforts at mutual adjustment and reconciliation had failed. Thus a fine balance always existed between life, on the one hand, which stressed the permanence of marriage, and the law, on the other, which had a remedy available when the basis for the marriage collapsed.

In modern times, with the rise of promiscuity, illegitimate births, and abortions, and with the breakdown of traditional standards of morality within the marriage union, there has been a great increase in the incidence of divorce in Jewish life. For Jews, this represents a serious problem since they no longer have the determining voice on whether divorces shall be granted or not. Once the state has granted a divorce, it is incumbent upon the religious community to recognize it and all too often, pro forma, an ecclesiastical divorce is granted. The task of Jewish religious leadership consists in trying to effect an ethical revival in this generation through the educational processes, by teaching and preaching the religious attitude to marriage, as a compact in which not two, but three, partners are involved, man, woman, and God. The Rabbis of old produced an ingenious homily on this theme: The Hebrew word *Ish,* "man" contains the letter *"yod"* which is missing from the word *Ishah,* "woman," but the word *Ishah* contains the letter *'heh"* which is missing in the word *Ish.* When these two words are joined together—the *"yod"* and *"heh"* are brought together and spell the word *Yah* which is the Hebrew name for God. On the other hand, if you remove the two letters from *Ish* and *Ishah,* you are left with the word *Esh,* fire. The moral is clear: when the marriage is a true union of body and spirit in which husband and wife are bound together by a sacred duty, then God is their partner, the *Shekhinah* dwells in their midst. But when the sacredness has gone out of the marriage, that is, when *Yah* has been removed, then they are both transformed into consuming fires.

In this crucial area of human relationships we believe the insights of Judaism in matters of sex and marriage and divorce offer light and guidance to our confused and bewildered generation.

II

ETHICS OF ROMAN CATHOLICISM

JOSEPH P. FITZPATRICK, S.J.

Associate Professor of Sociology
Fordham University

I must begin with a word of sincere thanks to Professor Johnson for inviting me to speak in this course, and for giving me the privilege of discussing with you, in my own inadequate way, how a Catholic approaches the responsibility of moral decision. I am sure that Professor Johnson realized that an adequate discussion of this topic would be an impossible task. But, I shall try 1) to sketch briefly the orientation of the ordinary Catholic to moral decision; and 2) to examine some of the implications of changing social conditions for moral values and moral decisions.

I

Professor Johnson has asked us to keep in mind, during our discussions, two major difficulties: one, the fact that deeply religious men differ about the norms of human behavior; secondly, the fact that all traditional norms of human behavior are being challenged today by men who hope to replace traditional morality by scientific conclusions as a guide to human conduct. The first difficulty is all the more serious because the second is threatening. In fact, it is precisely the first difficulty, the division among religious men, that has to some extent provoked the second, namely, the impatience of the scientist with moral leaders who fail to agree on moral issues, and his tendency to cry, "A plague on both your houses," as he seeks for certainty by the method of empirical inquiry.

With reference to the first difficulty, I take it that the aim of this series is to provide a presentation of moral principles outside of a context of conflict in which opposing norms become the rallying points of opposing camps, symbols of loyalty to the in-group. It aims to provide a presentation of moral principles for the calm examination of sincere and intelligent men. This would do three things: sharpen our awareness of moral principles in general, disclose the principles on which there is agreement, clarify the principles on which there is difference and the reasons why the difference prevails. With the help of God, this would lead men closer to the truth.

With reference to the second difficulty, the course apparently is expected to provide a reassertion of the main principles of traditional morality: the insistence on a transcendent moral order, the ability of men to know the moral law, and the primacy of moral norms in human behavior. It will also allow for an examination of the vexing questions that modern science, particularly the behavioral sciences, are raising about moral values. Actually modern science, when looked at carefully, can contribute a good deal to a sharpening of our understanding of moral decision. Psychology and psychiatry have enabled us to define much more carefully the limits of human freedom in human action; and sociology and anthropology have enabled us to clarify the manner in which particular cultures define what is right and what is wrong.

It is obvious that what Professor Johnson is after is not theoretical analysis of the derivation of moral norms as this would be presented in a textbook; he wants to get at the experience of the human person in determining his own behavior in actual situations, that is, moral decision in process. This takes us beyond the philosophical and theological question of moral principles and involves us in the psychology of actual moral behavior. What man ought to do and what he actually does are two quite different things. What, therefore, is the value of a moral principle if it does not effectively guide the behavior of men? One sees reflected in the question of the course the anxious striving of modern men for a realistic and meaningful morality.

Involved in this question are two problems: one, the classic problem of good and evil, of right and wrong. Men have been universally consistent in condemning certain acts as evil, and equally consistent in doing the evil acts that they condemn. The problem of how to bring men to do that which is good has been with us since the days of Adam. It is not a problem which is specific to our times; it is now simply more complicated. Therefore, it seems to me that any proposal that science will eliminate the struggle between good and evil in men's lives by substituting a "scientific ethic," or a "scientific method of determining human behavior," need not delay our discussion. It seems to imply that, in order to do what is right, all a man needs is to know what is right. In this matter, the record of human history is too eloquent, and the expression of human experience is too loud and clear to be denied.

The second problem, the real problem as it is suggested in the prospectus of this course, lies elsewhere. It is the problem of good men who acknowledge within themselves the struggle of good and evil, but who do not entirely agree on what is good and what is evil. Or when they do agree in principle on what is good or evil, right or wrong, they do not agree in the application of the principle to particular cases. Finally, when there is widespread agreement on what is right and wrong, the problem we have just mentioned comes to the fore, *i.e.*, the failure of many men to do what is generally considered right.

It would not be entirely accurate to associate these differences with differences of religious faith, as if they did not occur among people with the same religious faith. It is true, for instance, that a number of moral principles are taught authoritatively by the Catholic Church, and later on we shall examine the role of the Church's authority in this area. These principles provide secure guidance to moral decision in many instances, but there are many situations in which one would look in vain for uniformity of moral decision among Catholics, difficult situations in which moral decisions cannot easily be reached by reference to general moral principles. One group of Catholics may campaign for right-to-work laws while another group is violently opposed to them; the American Bishops issue a statement about the immorality of segregation, but thousands of Catholics continue to defend it; nations prepare for nuclear warfare while Catholics remain uncertain about approving or condemning it. It appears, therefore, that the problem of moral decision in many issues is as difficult for Catholics as it is for men of any faith. And this, I take it, is the issue on which our discussion should be centered: What is the source of moral norms; how do men determine what is right and wrong? And, once having determined this, how do men set about to make these norms effective?

The Catholic approaches moral decision as one who lives at one moment in a great and dramatic historical process: the process of God's redemption of the world. God had created man to His own image, had endowed him with the remarkable gift of reason, and had placed in man's hands the power to determine his own destiny by his own freedom. When man misused his freedom and brought disorder into his life, God, instead of abandoning him, promised to redeem him. He spoke to him repeatedly through the prophets, and, finally, came into the world in the person of His Divine Son, shared our life, died in order to save us, rose from the dead and ascended into heaven where, if we have remained faithful to Him, He will glorify us. Therefore, the Catholic approach to morality is influenced by these profoundly moving convictions: that man, by his reason can know what is right and can guide his moral behavior accordingly; that God has spoken to man and, therefore, man can learn with certainty what God has told him; that God is a God of mercy and forgiveness.

Within this framework of Catholic belief, two sources of moral norms have always been recognized. The first one is the nature of man himself as a rational creature. Man's reason, functioning normally and naturally, should recognize man's destiny, man's innate power to reach that destiny, and the things that man must do in order to achieve that destiny. Man, alone among the creatures of the earth, has intellectual knowledge; man, alone of all the creatures of the earth, conceives his acts in terms of obligation. He does not only say, "I do," or "I do not": he says, "I ought," and "I ought not." The basic principles of morality, therefore, are not the characteristics of a particular religious faith. They are the norms, universally recognized, by reasoning men: do good and avoid evil; thou shalt not wantonly kill another man; care for the children you have begotten; respect the aged; reverence the dead, etc.

This is always referred to in Catholic tradition as moral philosophy; as ethics. Consequently, there is no such thing as Catholic ethics; there is simply ethics—the moral norms which all men should share because they are endowed with the same nature. These moral norms constitute what is known as the natural moral law. Rooted in the common nature which all men share, recognized by the human reason that guides man's conduct, the natural moral law should be the universal norm for the conduct of men everywhere.

The failure of men to acknowledge the natural law, or their failure to observe it when they do acknowledge it, is eloquently written in the tragedies of man's history. Even more eloquently written, however, is man's struggle to know it and observe it by transcending his selfishness in moments of altruism, by overcoming tyranny in conquests of freedom, by the constant struggle for order in his life, by his respect for others and his demand for respect in return.

There is a second source of moral norms characteristic of the Catholic tradition: the firm belief that God has established a relationship between Himself and men that transcends nature; has established an order of things in which man, through grace, can participate in the life of God, can perform acts which will enable him to enjoy a union with God that could never be achieved by his natural powers as a man. This relationship of man to God is called, in Catholic theology, the supernatural life. It is the way of salvation, given to men through Jesus Christ, and the truths pertaining to salvation and taught to us by Jesus Christ constitute the data of revelation. "Amen, amen I say to thee unless thou art born again of water and the Holy Spirit, thou canst not enter into the Kingdom of God" (Jn. 3/3), "Unless you eat the flesh of the Son of Man and drink His Blood, you shall not have life in you" (Jn. 6/54), are principles directing the behavior of men toward a supernatural life. Man could know these things only if God had told him.

In this order of revelation, it is clear that the Catholic Church teaches a great many principles that guide the behavior of men; these teachings are explicitly religious and many of them are explicitly Catholic. Therefore, in discussing "patterns of ethics among Catholics" it is extremely important that this distinction be kept clear between principles of natural morality which pertain to all men and are available to man's natural reason, and the principles of behavior that pertain directly to salvation and have been positively revealed by God in the person of Jesus Christ. "Thou shalt not kill," or "Thou shalt not commit adultery" are principles of behavior that all men can recognize by their own reason. But the need for baptism, and the Eucharist; the counsel of virginity as a state more perfect than marriage; the principle that good works can merit grace, these are principles that man could not have known by his own reason.

However, the way of salvation, the supernatural life does not disregard the order of natural morality. It presupposes it. Therefore, Jesus Christ not only taught us the truths that pertain to the supernatural life, He clarified many of the norms of ethics; explained decisively what man could have known by nature. As a result, under the guidance of revelation, man sees much more clearly the principles of natural morality which may have been obscure before. If anything could be called a Catholic ethics, distinct from revealed norms of behavior, it could be this: the principles of natural morality, clarified, strengthened and explained by God's positive word to man. What previously had been doubtful now becomes certain; what previously had been vague, now becomes sharp in outline; what previously had been unconvincing, now becomes convincing. Man, under the inspiration of faith and grace becomes sure of himself.

Therefore the thing that gives the firmness and security to moral teaching among Catholics remains the word of God, spoken to men in the Person of the Savior, Jesus Christ, whether this was His word revealing supernatural truths, or reinforcing the truths of natural morality. "Amen, amen, I say to you, he that loveth Me, shall keep my commandments" (Jn. 14/15). However, if God came into the world in order to teach men truth, it is quite obvious to the Catholic that He would take the necessary means to enable all men to receive His word, uncorrupted, clear, definite. He did this by establishing a Church and conferring upon it the authority to teach His word without error. "Going therefore, teach ye all nations, baptizing them, etc., teaching them to observe and do whatsoever I have commanded you" (Mt. 28/19–20). "Whatsoever you shall bind on earth shall be bound in heaven; whatsoever you shall loose upon earth, shall be loosed in Heaven" (Mt. 16/19). "I shall be with you all days unto the end of the world" (Mt. 28/20).

This, then, I would say is the specific character of the Catholic's approach to moral decision, that he recognizes one source of final moral authority in this world that speaks with the authority of God Himself. This authority is the teaching Church, particularly the authority of the Supreme Pontiff, the Vicar of Christ on earth, the Pope, at those moments when he is authoritatively teaching a doctrine of faith and morals.

One important note should be added at this point, namely, that not every moral principle is taught by the Catholic Church with the same degree of insistence on its truth. Some principles are formally defined as having been revealed as true, such as the need for baptism; others are commonly accepted as having been revealed, still others may be acknowledged to be only probable. It is the constant effort of theologians to clarify the degree of certainty with which a truth is taught as part of revelation.

However, with reference to the principles of natural morality, the Church simply teaches these as principles which are evident to human reason. That a man should not wantonly injure a neighbor or kill him; that a man should not steal or commit adultery, are truths that are taught as part of natural morality. However, even on this level, differences may appear. The principle that contraception is immoral is taught with such insistence by the Church that no one would be permitted to teach anything to the contrary. On the other hand, circumstances which justify the use of rhythm by a married couple have been a matter of considerable controversy.

I trust that this will provide a brief but clear idea of the manner in which Catholics derive their knowledge of moral principles.

The determination of the general moral principle, however, is only the first step in the difficult process of arriving at moral decision. It is extremely helpful to the Catholic that, in many moral matters, he knows with certainty what the moral norm is. It is clear also that, in many moral matters, he, like the sincere men outside his faith, still finds it difficult to arrive at moral decision.

The second step is to determine how a general moral norm applies in a particular situation. There are some situations, such as the committing of adultery, in which the application of the principle is obvious and clear. There are other situations where the clarification of the principle makes its application rather obvious also, such as the clear teaching that direct abortion is the taking of life, and therefore is morally forbidden under any circumstances. But many of the situations which face us today are not simple at all and, regardless of how clearly the principle may be taught, the application of the principle to complicated situations is extremely difficult. This is the troublesome area in moral decision in which understanding, insight, prudence, and courage play such a critical role. It is the perception of the application of the general norm to a difficult situation that marks the great judge, the great counselor, the great saint. For example, I accept the principle that every man must be just. But what is justice? I am told that justice is the virtue by which I give every man that which is his due. But what is due to this man or that? Suppose I accept the principle that it is moral to defend myself in a defensive war. But if one waits to be attacked in a nuclear war, no defense will be possible.

And with modern weapons is all war unjust because the consequences will almost surely be worse than the situation the war was supposed to correct? Let us agree that men have the right to work since work is the only means of livelihood. But if a man's insistence on his right will weaken the union that protects a thousand other men, can he justly insist on it? Let us agree that segregation is unjust; may I resort to methods of desegregation which may lead to greater evils than the segregation itself?

This, I think we will all agree, is the problem area of moral decision. How do men determine the particular application of a general norm? St. Thomas once made the remark that only the just man could really say what was the just thing to do in a particular matter. In other words, it is the virtuous life, the constant striving of a man for justice or charity, that cultivates in him the disposition to recognize what is just or charitable in a difficult situation; that enables him to overcome the tendency to rationalize his own selfishness; that strengthens him to make the sacrifice that justice or charity would demand.

Fortunately, there are not a few virtuous men in the world, and what generally results is a consensus of sincere men of goodwill as to what is right or wrong in a particular situation, as to what is the prudent or imprudent thing to do. The almost universal condemnation of slavery that has developed during the past century; the resistance to child labor in industrial and commercial areas; the insistence on educational opportunities; these are a few examples of decisions which men have come, in increasing numbers, to acknowledge as right.

But there will continue to be numerous situations where even the just man will find it difficult to arrive at a just judgment. In a rapidly changing world, it may be impossible to gather sufficient information; or by the time information has been gathered, the situation has changed; or we may be confronted with situations where no just alternatives are possible and we must resort to the lesser of two evils. In these situations, we try to arrive at the most just possible decision, respecting always the person of our opponents while we find it necessary to disagree with them.

In this whole matter of applying a general norm to particular cases, is there a specifically Catholic orientation to moral decision? I doubt it. The Catholic enjoys the security of a moral authority which gives him the assurance of truth in many of his general moral norms; he may also receive the guidance of the moral authority of the Church in some practical applications. But, for the most part, in arriving at particular decisions, he will find himself experiencing the same distress of virtuous men everywhere who strive to do what is right while they realize that in many cases they feel their way along uncertain pathways. If anyone has the impression that the doctrine of the natural moral law, and the belief in the moral authority of the Church provide the Catholic with a push-button morality, he has surely never known the anxiety that Catholics experience as they try to arrive at judgments of prudence and justice.

Now I would like to say a few words about the third step in moral decision, the moral action itself. Situational ethics tend to remove the emphasis from objective values and norms and place it on the existing situation, giving the impression that each particular act has its own morality—what the person thinks is moral in that situation. Before commenting on this, it will help to recall that, in the Catholic tradition, together with the firm emphasis on certain and objective norms of morality, there has always been a clear recognition that circumstances modify the character of an action. Most important of all in actual behavior is the person's state of mind, whether he knows what he is doing is right or wrong. The ultimate test of personal guilt or innocence lies not in the objective norm of right or wrong; it is in the person's conscience. If a person is sincerely convinced that what he is doing is right, he may be doing a hideous thing, but he is virtuous in doing it. If a person considers an action to be right, he is morally obliged to do it even though it be objectively wrong; if a person considers an action to be wrong, he is forbidden to do it even though it be objectively right. One of the great influences of Christianity was precisely in this emphasis that good and evil were not simply a matter of conserving or disrupting an objective order of things; they were much more a matter of a man's state of mind as he determined his own actions.

The great caution necessary here is quite obvious. The fact that a person thinks an action is right does not make it right. All moral education is aimed at instructing the individual to recognize the objective norm which should govern his behavior. This is the difficult task of moral teaching and moral learning. The norm of morality is objective; it transcends the individual will. Otherwise order would be impossible.

Moreover, the Church has always emphasized the influence of other circumstances on a person's behavior. Morality is an objective norm, but the people who try to conform to the norm are living, human persons, with all the pressures and difficulties and weaknesses of people living among their fellows. It is perfectly possible for a person to know that adultery is wrong but in a moment of great weakness, or under powerful pressures, he may do that which he knows to be wrong. Circumstances sometimes make it almost humanly impossible for a person to do that which he knows he should do. This does not imply that the norm should be changed to fit the demands of the situation; it means that all must be done to cultivate the strength that is necessary to do what is right, and to create a social situation in which doing what is right becomes possible if not easy.

With reference to these actual situations, the Catholic approaches moral decision with the firm conviction that God is infinitely merciful as well as infinitely just. Together with His firm emphasis on moral norms, our Savior gave a remarkable example of forgiveness. "How many times shall I forgive my brother," asked Peter, "seven times?" "Amen I say to you, seventy times seven," was the Lord's answer. In the light of this perhaps one can begin to understand what appears sometimes as a puzzling contradiction in the Catholic Church: what appears to be an extreme rigidity of moral principle together with what appears to be an extreme of tolerance for human weakness in dealing with the individual sinner.

This indicates once again the deep concern of the Church, while insisting on the moral norms, to take into account every aspect of the situation in which the individual is acting.

Finally, in this general part of the discussion, I would like to say a word about sanctions. The only sanctions that operate among Catholics on the level of natural morality, are the moral sanctions of the natural law: the human perfection which follows from moral goodness, and the human failure which follows upon moral evil; the ultimate end of happiness in the life to come which is the reward of a morally good life, and the ultimate end of punishment in the life to come which is the end of a morally evil life.

There appears to be an opinion that the Catholic Church exercises the sanction of excommunication in attempting to enforce the norms of behavior. Excommunication is a sanction, but it applies in rare cases, and could never be considered an ordinary means of enforcing moral behavior. It is a disciplinary measure applied generally where there is some public danger to the Church or to the faithful. The Holy Father, for instance, if danger to the Church seemed to warrant it, could forbid the faithful, under the pain of excommunication, to join certain associations; or a Bishop, in similar circumstances, could forbid the Catholics of his diocese, under pain of excommunication, to attend a certain theater, to participate in certain forms of political activity. Excommunication is a penalty which separates the member of the Church from communion with the rest of the faithful, either by denying him access to the sacraments such as penance or the Eucharist, or, in a very rare and extreme case, by forbidding members of the Church to associate with him at all. When the offender has fulfilled the proper conditions, the excommunication is removed either by the one who imposed it, or, more generally, by a priest who has been granted the power to remove it. However, in the ordinary efforts of the Church to guide her children to a good and virtuous life, excommunication as a sanction is not an important issue. A person could commit adultery many times and never be excommunicated; could disregard serious obligations to parents or children; could be a very unjust employer or employe; could engage in forms of corruption in public office; a person, in short, could lead a very immoral and unholy life and never incur excommunication. In confession, it is true, the confessor can grant absolution only when he is confident that the penitent is determined to avoid sinning in the future, and refusal of absolution to an habitual sinner will prevent his participation in communion. But it is evident that this is a moral sanction, and not a matter of excommunication.

Consequently, in the effort to bring men to the practice of a good moral life, the sanctions of the Catholic Church in enforcing moral principles are of the same nature as moral sanctions among all men; the appeal to man's higher nature, to his desire for perfection, to his effort to reach eternal happiness.

II

With the foregoing remarks as a background, it is possible to examine some of the factors which influence moral decision; the context of moral judgment which can create difficulties for Catholics as for people of other faiths. The particular factors which I wish to examine in some detail are the cultural and social factors which become involved in moral judgment. In this area the development of the social sciences has rather serious implications for the moral teacher.

Morality, if it is to mean anything, must be relevant. But, in order to be relevant, it must be relative to situations that a person is facing. It is the failure to recognize this that can give to many general moral statements, whether by Catholics or others, an air of unreality. A person can know the situation only if he has sufficient insight into the culture, and sufficient knowledge of the social and economic organization. It is this insight into the culture by which a person perceives what a situation means to the members of that culture, and it is only in terms of those meanings that moral judgment can be relevant. In India, the parents of a girl are expected to choose her marriage partner for her. If American parents attempted to do the same thing for a modern American girl, it would be considered a serious violation of the girl's rights.

The isolation of the aged which is taken for granted in American culture, would be considered sinfully disrespectful in traditional Chinese families. It was possible for deeply spiritual and moral men to consider slavery acceptable in the thirteenth century; men like them consider it morally abhorrent in the twentieth. It was quite ethical for a father to leave a child illiterate in the seventeenth century, whereas the American father who did so today would be failing in one of his most serious moral responsibilities. The reason is clear: an illiterate man two centuries ago could function effectively as an active and influential man in his community, whereas in the contemporary United States an illiterate man is hopelessly handicapped. It is the culture and the social situation that reveal the real significance of a fact or practice such as illiteracy or the treatment of the aged; it is the culture that outlines the context in which moral judgment becomes relevant.

It is easier to recognize this in matters of social and economic organization than in more subtle matters of culture. One of the classic examples is the history of the attempts during the past century to pass minimum wage laws in the United States. In a number of cases, minimum wage laws were declared unconstitutional by the Supreme Court on the ground that they interfered with the freedom of contract guaranteed by the Constitution of the United States. In this legal matter, there were certainly moral judgments involved based on the principle that free men must be guaranteed the right to make free contracts. If a New York laundress wanted to make a free contract to work for two cents an hour, the state had no recognized right to interfere with her freedom. This kind of moral reasoning may have been applicable in the case of independent New England farmers in the year 1800. But when it came to poverty-stricken immigrants underbidding each other pitifully for desperately needed jobs, such a wage agreement was not a matter of economic freedom, but of economic slavery. Prudent moral judgment in the circumstances, therefore, required a knowledge of the facts and an insight into the meaning of the facts. This would have enabled one to pass judgment realistically upon the situation.

The endless ramifications of these social and economic changes are extremely important for the man faced with ethical decisions. To the Puerto Rican farmer, the competitiveness of Americans in business and economic life seems like an inhuman lack of charity and consideration for one's friends and neighbors; to the competitive American, the family loyalties of the Puerto Rican are judged to be a kind of laziness and lack of responsibility. In both cases, a moral judgment is being made, but it can be made realistically only in relation to the meaning that certain facts have for the people of certain cultures.

It is even more difficult to understand the meaning things have in more subtle aspects of a culture. I suppose that nothing so much as the question of modesty reveals the importance of cultural definitions. Some of the poor families in Puerto Rico leave the little boys unclothed. If Puerto Rican mothers continue this practice in New York, older New Yorkers frequently accuse them of being indecent. We take it for granted in the United States that men or boys, using a swimming pool in a protected situation, will swim together in the nude. In fact, we would probably be a bit concerned about a boy or young man who was reluctant to do this. But this practice would be considered very immoral by men of many other cultures. The old Japanese practice of the entire family, men, women, and children bathing together naked in the public baths, is something that we would define as immoral in our American culture. Father André Dupeyrat, in his account of the Papuans, tells a vivid story of a Papuan woman, wearing nothing but a slight loin cloth that left her practically naked. Yet when her husband quarreled publicly with her and suddenly tore off the loin cloth, the woman's sense of shame was so outraged that she climbed a nearby tree and cast herself to her death on the rocks below. Father Dupeyrat uses this as an illustration of the importance of knowing the cultural definitions of what is modest and what is not before one passes judgment upon them.

These remarks do not suggest a case for cultural determinism. Moral norms are not the functional resultant of culture patterns. All the anthropology in the world will never convince a universe of morally minded men that the killing of the aged by the Papuans is objectively right, however much the Papuans may think it is. What I have in mind, rather, are those principles particularly of justice, of charity, of modesty, of interpersonal relations involving respect or insult, etc.—principles which an individual can apply only by taking cognizance of the significance that situations have for the members of the culture that are engaged in them. *Ex factis oritur jus* is the saying. The facts reveal the actual relationship which is either just or unjust, and it is only by knowing the significance of the relationship that one can judge it to be either just or unjust. Many a middle class American family, with its emphasis on external show of affection, would consider the coolness and aloofness of many a father in traditional families to be quite inhuman; might even judge it as failure to observe the moral duty to love one's children. They would not perceive that right and obligation in these traditional families are centered on such things as respect, recognition of one's status, acknowledgment of one's achievements. External show of affection is dismissed as trivial, which perhaps in the long run it may be.

It is helpful to keep these points in mind since the failure to take account of these cultural factors has frequently led first to differences in the moral judgments that were passed and secondly to a kind of moral judgment that is quite unrealistic. With these considerations in mind, we can proceed to some of the concrete questions that have been posed from this platform.

III

Economic issues

When a person seeks to clarify the moral issues involved in the relationship of government initiative and free enterprise, he must cope with a host of complicated factors in a social and economic system. Moral judgment in this area becomes extremely complicated because of 1) the difficulty of knowing the important facts; 2) the difficulty of knowing what the facts mean when we do have them; 3) the difficulty of determining prudently the best ethical policy if we do know that the facts signify an unjust situation. One who has followed any of the great public controversies such as the one concerning T.V.A., or the right of the States to dispose of off-shore oil resources, or anti-trust decisions, cannot help being bewildered at the enormous amounts of conflicting data that are presented. Secondly, with reference to the meaning of the facts, to speak of free enterprise in India the way we speak about it in the United States makes very little sense. The general moral principles of private property require considerable qualification if they are used in judgment of ten shares of General Motors stock belonging to a broker; ten head of cattle belonging to a Bantu tribesman; or ten acres of land belonging to an Irish countryman. But one does not have to look at other cultures; even within the United States, the same moral principles must be qualified in relation to the new meaning things have in our rapidly changing social and economic organization. The development of atomic energy is quite different from the gold rush; and explorations into space are worlds apart from homesteading. Finally, when we do perceive rather clearly the significance of economic and social facts, moral decision may be extremely difficult. A farm policy that pays farmers handsome sums of money not to grow food in a world in which millions are starving appears to be a poor way to deal with economic disorders. But the conscientious leader would not find it easy to reach a workable policy closer to our ideals of justice.

The Catholic approach to moral decisions in this area of social and economic life is ordinarily based on principles of natural morality, that is, principles which men of goodwill should be able to recognize by considering the nature of man and the nature of economic activity. God has placed in man's hands the freedom and the power to develop and perfect himself. But man can develop his perfection only by the use of the material goods of the world. Therefore he has a right to the goods which he needs for his own perfection. The air we breathe, the spring of cooling water, the lake alive with fish, the pasture nourishing the patient flock—God had intended these for all men. All men, therefore, should have adequate access to them—and, if they organize themselves politically, it is the function of their government to do all that is necessary to assure them adequate access to the goods they need; in other words, to promote the common welfare. The idea that "That State governs best which governs least" was never an accepted principle in the philosophy of Catholic thinkers about the State. I emphasize philosophy because theology and revelation have little to say formally about social or political organization.

Therefore when the question of ethical decision arises about how much "government initiative" is necessary in economic life, teachers in the Catholic tradition would reply: "Whatever initiative is necessary to promote the general welfare." This dismisses anything like a *laissez-faire* government, to be sure, but it does not help us much in determining what kind of government initiative is necessary and how much. This is where the question of fact arises; and the question of what the facts signify; and the question of what is the prudent thing to do in the presence of facts that mean what these mean. This is where the well-informed man is so important—first, the man who knows the facts of the economic and social order; secondly, the man who has the insight to perceive the significance of the facts; thirdly, the just man who has the disposition to justice and who can judge what is just or prudent in particular situations. Some questions of government initiative are so clear that most people spontaneously recognize them; for example, the need for pure food laws, and the prevention of the wanton exploitation of natural resources. Other questions become clear over a period of time, such as social security legislation. No intelligent man of integrity would question today the necessity of social security; but thirty years ago, millions of such men would have opposed it. Finally, there are the complicated issues where controversy still prevails, such as whether the government should exploit the natural resources that belong to the people, or market the power generated at the great public power dams.

In all these issues, the remarks I have made previously have great pertinence. What do facts mean in a given economic or social order? There is no perfect social or economic order. Strictly speaking, there is no "Catholic social order," or "Christian social order."

We use these terms to describe a social and economic order in which the behavior of men is guided by Catholic ideals or Christian principles. This would be a social order which men of sincere moral principles and great integrity believe is the best expression of justice and charity that is possible at a given time in given circumstances.

Marriage and family life

The second area suggested to us for discussion was that of family life. This is an area where moral issues are much clearer than in economic life. The fact that they are clearer does not make them less controversial. In fact, because the issues are clearer, and morality touches individuals so intimately, differences of opinion in matters of family morality tend to become involved in more vehement controversy. Generally, it is a little easier to get at matters between husband and wife than at matters between employers and employees or between two great world powers. Here, in the matter of marriage, moral decision is more precise, and revelation and theology have a much more decisive role to play. Our Lord never said, "Workmen shall never strike against their masters." But He did say "What God hath joined together, let no man put asunder." God has manifested a much more direct and positive concern about the matter of marriage and family life than about government intervention in economic activities.

Catholics approach decisions concerning marriage and family life definitely with a religious orientation. Catholics believe that God has raised marriage to the dignity of a sacrament—made of the union of husband and wife a means of supernatural grace. As one reads the fifth chapter of *Ephesians,* he sees the exalted ideal of Christian marriage, the union of man and woman that is like the union of Christ with His Church—wife bringing spiritual perfection to husband and husband to wife. I realize fully that millions of Catholics have little awareness of this ideal and experience little of its fulfilment in their married lives. But it does set the framework within which decisions should be made, and actually are made by millions of others who are aware of the "mystery."

Ethical decisions about marriage, therefore, are set within the context of very high religious ideals. Men and women marry to achieve, with God's grace, a union between themselves that is like the union of Christ with His Church, to sanctify each other, to procreate and bring up children to the Lord. But moral decisions concerning marriage are likewise set within the context of different cultures, and the cultural factor plays a very large part. For instance, shall husband and wife freely choose each other after a period of courtship and romantic love, as in the United States, or should the families arrange the marriage, as in India? Is one of these ways the "Catholic way" while the other is not? Not at all. These are cultural practices within which the ideal of Catholic marriage may be sought. It is as dangerous for American Catholics to identify their cultural practices with Catholic marriage as it would be for the Catholics of India to identify it with theirs. Nevertheless, the cultural context does have a serious influence on moral decision. An Indian parent who told his daughter to go out and meet some men and find a husband for herself would definitely be judged to be failing in one of his serious moral obligations to his daughter; whereas an American parent who insisted that his daughter marry the young man the parent chose would be judged to be disregarding one of the most important moral rights of his daughter. After a couple are married, is the Catholic ideal to be realized by keeping the woman subordinate to the husband, subject to his word, economically dependent; or is it realized by a more cooperative relationship in which the husband consults the wife and she has a measure of economic equality? In neither essentially. These are cultural practices and, within the framework of each, the Catholic ideal can be sought. What is important in relation to moral decisions is that a man keep in mind the entire cultural context lest he define his own cultural practices as if they were moral absolutes.

But one need not go to other cultures to examine the relationship of moral principles to different cultural situations. Within our own American society, cultural changes must be kept in mind when moral decisions are being made. Women, for instance, have always played a large part in the economic activities of the home;

but, in a rural economy, her work was in the vicinity of the home and was geared to family relationships. The rapidly changing technology of our society, the widespread urbanization of our people (70 per cent now live in urban areas) have led to a situation where the woman's contribution to the economic activity of the home can be fulfilled only by working for a wage outside the home. As a result, 30 per cent of all married women are gainfully employed. The working mother has come in for an abundant share of moral judgments, but not all of these have been made with an understanding of the changing sociological factors that seriously affect her life, and which must be kept in mind if moral decisions concerning her are to be relevant.

Celibacy

It is within the context of the high religious ideals toward family life that the meaning of virginity and celibacy among Catholics becomes clear. This ideal, the positive consecration of one's life to God, and the forgoing of marriage with its intimate union with another person, its legitimate sexual expression, its fulfilment of self in the generation of children, is indeed a great mystery. It is the profound mystery of men and women who honor God by never using the greatest physical power God has given them, the power to beget and bear children. It is a mystery based not on natural morality, but on revelation. Our Lord's praise for those who would remain unmarried for the sake of the Kingdom of Heaven (Mt. 19/12); St. Paul's praise of virginity as leaving a person free to dedicate himself to the things of the Lord (I Cor. 7/32–33); and the long, clear tradition of the Church have led to a respect for virginity, chosen out of love for God, as a state of great perfection. Therefore, the emphasis on the moral value of a life of celibacy has never been the result of a revolt against sex or a flight from marriage as evil. Presupposing a great reverence for marriage, the Catholic emphasis on virginity recognizes that men and women honor God more by sacrificing a state that would be a fulfilment for themselves and a great honor to God, in order to seek a more perfect imitation of Christ. Therefore celibacy is encouraged not because celibacy is good and marriage bad; but because, while marriage is a great good, celibacy is a greater good.

Divorce and contraception

The next specific points for discussion bring us into rather controversial areas. A number of positive doctrines concerning marriage are taught very firmly by the Church; *i.e.,* that a valid sacramental, consummated marriage cannot be dissolved; that marriage exists primarily for the procreation and nourishment of children; that manipulation of sexual relations in order to prevent the natural consequences of these relations is immoral.

Each of these doctrines would require an entire paper for itself. These moral principles, that divorce and contraception are violations of God's law, touch people very intimately, and the position of the Church is too well known to need elaboration. What is helpful is perspective, some idea of the state of mind, as it were, of Catholic leaders and teachers when they assert these doctrines.

No Catholic, more importantly no Catholic leader, is unaware of the difficulties these principles present to Catholic people at the present time. Why, then, does the Church continue to insist on them as principles for moral decision? The Church certainly loves her children, and does not wish to inflict suffering on them. But she insists upon these principles because, in the framework of her life and teaching, she cannot escape the conviction that these are the laws of God and she must instruct men that they must direct their lives in accordance with them. The Church sees these principles as part of the all-embracing vision of man's perfection that God has planned and, if they are accepted with this state of mind, they can help man to rise to the heights of perfection and development that God had planned for him.

Ordinarily the moral principles concerning divorce and contraception are presented in discussion by Catholics as principles of the natural moral law, that is, they should be clear to right minded men who know the nature of man. This is true, theoretically. But in the order of practical decision, the basis for the firm conviction of Catholics with regard to these two principles is not the clarity of the natural law but the authority of the Church. This is one clear case where principles of natural morality are clarified by faith. It is perfectly obvious to Catholics that most serious thinkers who are not Catholics, many of them men of deep and sincere religious lives, do not agree that contraception is immoral. It cannot be as clear a principle of the natural moral law as some Catholic writers sometimes make it out to be. Without faith in the authority of the Church in this matter, conviction would be weaker than it is.

It is unfortunate that discussions of contraception become so heated and bitter. This is probably inevitable since it touches so directly on the intimate relations of individuals in their personal lives, and on questions of policy in public life. But it obscures the fact that the matter of contraception is quite subordinate to a whole framework of spiritual and religious values pertaining to marriage; and, in matters of public policy concerning population, it is related to a badly disorganized economic and political order of things, and a number of mysteries concerning the future. The primary objective of Catholics, as it undoubtedly is of many other religious people, is to cultivate in the people of the world a knowledge and acceptance of the deep meaning of marriage and the family, a level of spiritual perfection that will enable them to keep the physical aspects of sexual behavior properly related to the great purposes for which God instituted marriage and for which Christ exalted it.

Catholics have no illusions as to the large number of their own who fail in the matter of contraception. But moral failure, particularly in matters of sex, is no surprise to the Church. Nor does the truth of a moral principle or a spiritual ideal depend on the number of people who observe it. What is more impressive than the failures is the rapidly increasing number of people, advancing in their knowledge of the faith and their devotion to its ideals, who are bringing to their family life a spiritual vigor that promises well for the future of the Church and our society.

I hope that this discussion has communicated some clear ideas of the factors involved in moral and ethical decisions as they are faced by Catholics. Catholics are fortunate in having the secure guideposts of their faith, and of principles of natural morality that are supported by their faith. In many situations their approach to moral decision is confident and secure. But in many other situations they face the same difficulties as all other men of goodwill who must attempt to determine the morality of complicated situations. I have tried in this paper to center my attention mainly on the difficulties that can be created for people if they are not alert to the cultural and social factors which must be carefully considered in moral decision. Also, I have tried to summarize the main points that are involved in a Catholic's attempt to reach a sound moral decision in particular matters of economic life or family life.

I do hope this will lend some clarity to discussion, and enable people to appreciate in some degree the state of mind in which Catholics approach ethical decisions.

The thing I had most hoped to do I am afraid I have not succeeded in doing, namely, to convey something of the inner life, the devotion to Christ, the Spirit of justice and charity that move the heart of the sincere Catholic as he approaches moral and ethical decisions. Catholic life is not a series of formulas, not a rigid blueprint, nor a succession of prohibitions, although in the heat of controversy a defense of the Church's position may make it appear that way. Catholic life is the perpetuation of the life of Christ among us, the living out of God's great redemption in all of us, and the effort to extend that great grace to all. The Catholic is deeply aware that there is an order of nature established by God, and an order of redemption which has been effected by Christ. Man's perfection consists, therefore, in realizing within himself, with God's grace, the order which reflects the vision of his Creator and Redeemer. This order is not a vague and changing thing. Man can know it and, once he knows it, he makes himself like to God by observing it.

III

ETHICS OF PROTESTANTISM

A. T. MOLLEGEN

Professor of New Testament Languages and Literature,
Protestant Episcopal Theological Seminary
in Virginia

There is a Protestant ethics distinguishable from Roman Catholic ethics and from other religious and secular ethics. Unfortunately this fact does not mean that the unique Protestant ethics is easy to describe or that all individual Protestant Christians or Protestant bodies of Christians are in agreement about the nature of Protestant ethics. One only has to compare the ethical attitude toward religion in the public schools of the Protestants and Other Americans United for the Separation of Church and State, with the position of other Protestants to be clear about the lack of agreement in Protestantism. This difference merely illustrates a wide variety of ethical differences which characterizes the whole complex of Christian denominations that classify historically as Protestant. An attempt to discern an essential Protestant ethics is a risk for any interpreter. It, nevertheless, must be done if we are to have a section on Protestantism in a course on "Patterns of Ethics."

The uniqueness of Protestant ethics springs from the central Protestant experience, formulated theologically as "justification by faith" or even more tersely as "by faith alone." This is true despite the fact that perhaps the majority of American Protestants and a great many official Protestant denominations have been so cut off from their roots that they neither understand nor experience "justification by faith."

The symbolic language of justification by faith is personal, dramatic, and juridical. It means that God Who is personal, almighty and righteous has put His enemy, sinful man, into a right relationship with Himself despite man's unworthiness. This act of justification is concrete; it is done in history with an outward and visible historical aspect empirically accessible even to the unbeliever, namely, the fact of Jesus of Nazareth. Justification is what God has done for, to, and in man. This once and for all, unprecedented and unrepeatable deed is done by the coming of God as His rational self-manifestation (the Logos), as the Son of the Father, into unity with a complete and whole human nature, one who was and is Jesus of Nazareth, a first century Jew. Jesus, from his conception and forever, is man taken into unity with deity. Jesus is the Christ, the Logos become flesh (man), the eternal Son of God become incarnate. The justifying act is effected by God incarnate as Jesus, born, ministering and teaching, crucified and risen, at the right hand of God and communicating his Spirit (the Holy Spirit) to us. On the divine side there is the unexpected and incredible love of God acting on man. On the human side there is the free, fully human, historically conditioned person, Jesus, by whom God effects justification in the human and historical order. We may say that the humanity of the incarnate Son is instrumental in the divine action of justifying man, if instrumental does not imply any dehumanization or depersonalization of Jesus.

The impact of this action of divine justifying love evokes, in and from man, faith. Faith is human response to God's action of love toward man in Christ. It is the response of the whole man, rational soul and body (a psychosomatic response). It is the response of the human mind, will, and emotions. The responder trusts God in Christ, commits himself to God in Christ, and finds that obedience to God in Christ is not the loss of freedom to a tyrannical Lord but the perfecting of his own freedom. For God in Christ is one in "whose service is perfect freedom."

God's love in Christ evoking the faith response brings man into union with God, a union like that of a son with a father, of a wife with a husband, so that the whole power of God's personal influence flows through the union into the Christian. God as forth-going personal influence is God as Holy Spirit and since God's influence is through Christ, the Holy Spirit is Christ's Spirit, the Spirit which "proceedeth from the Father and (or through) the Son" (Nicene Creed). As Jesus, the historical man, was conceived by the Holy Spirit, so Christians are reborn by and into the Spirit. "Unless one is born of water and the Spirit, he cannot enter the kingdom of God," said the Johannine Christ to Nicodemus (Jn. 3:5).

According to justification-by-faith theology, both Christian moral character and Christian action in the world flow out of the new relationship to God. Moral goodness and moral action are not the precondition of right relationship to God but the result of such a right relationship. Grateful belonging to God is the motivation for moral effort. "We are not our own . . . we are God's," Calvin said in a kind of reiterated refrain in his *Institutes*.

Several things about this underlying Protestant experience are of especial interest here. First, neither the Church nor the state nor any historical institution can stand between men and God. No man and no group of men are united to God by their own worthiness but only by the undeserved merciful action of God in Christ, a justifying action received by faith. Only God is God, and the only man perfectly united to God dies upon a cross outside of Jerusalem. He does not reign from within history as a Davidic King, a ruler of this world, but from above history, as the crucified and risen Christ at the right hand of God.

This aspect of justification-by-faith theology has given Protestantism a theological ground from which to struggle against all authoritarianism, ecclesiastical or political, but it has also raised for Protestantism the insoluble problem of authority. The inability of Protestantism to resolve its problem of authority accounts for its fragmentation into many denominations and for its lack of agreement on the moral problems which we shall discuss later.

Secondly, the personal and living character of justification by faith and of receiving the Spirit gives Protestant ethics at its best a be-yond-but-not-below-the-law moral quality. One may phrase this in terms of the relationship of love, the fruit of the personal, living Holy Spirit, and Law, the attempt to define love as an obligation in the light of reason and the experience of the Church. As Jesus taught in the Sermon on the Mount (Matt. 5), the Law makes us know that love does not murder, commit adultery, divorce one's marital partner, perjure oneself or act with retaliation. Yet love is never exhausted by a series of rational injunctions or prohibitions and often is thrown in conflict with the Law insomuch as the Law expresses itself in prohibitions of, or injunctions to, overt actions. For instance, it is true that love does not murder and that the overt expression of murder is killing, but is it true that love never kills under any circumstances?

Thirdly, justification-by-faith theology at one and the same time takes away the possibility of man finding a good place above human society in which he may stand before God holy and unblemished, and immerses him responsibly in society itself. Neither the Church, nor the monastic orders, neither the mystical anchoritic life nor the sectarian cenobitic communities can be regarded as Christian alternatives to living responsibly in the world, in families, in local communities and in the whole stream of human history.

A Christian's calling (vocation) is not God's summons to leave social responsibility or to establish a community which is alongside of human society (except perhaps as a strategy for a special time). God's call is to live as a Christian responsibly related to family, to the economic order, to the cultural order, to the political order, and to the world situation in one's own time.

In brief, Protestantism sets individual man before God, justified and renewed but not good by his own merit, forbids him the comfort of any final creaturely authority, even that of the Law and his own conscience, commands him to love without his knowing beforehand exactly what love is to do, and holds him in responsibility to his historical existence without hope of escape to a better alternative until the second coming of Christ.

If this be even roughly true of the essence of Protestantism, one can see why it is impossible to define a Protestant pattern of ethics in terms of specific answers to the questions of "government initiative and private enterprise; the moral limits of the will to national survival; religious freedom for minority groups, particularly nonreligious minorities; and family life—*e.g.,* divorce, intermarriage, planned parenthood." But it is also true that we can describe a Protestant pattern of ethics in terms of some basic Protestant principles and attitudes which ought to characterize all Protestant approaches to these questions.

How, for instance, ought a Protestant to approach the question of the growth of a centralized federal government and its relation to the freedom of modern business institutions? This question has become increasingly harassing in the United States since 1930 and always appears as an important issue in all serious political discussions and political campaigns. One often hears sincere laments about government development toward tyrannical power over business life, over states' rights, over local autonomy in the public schools, and over the individual's private rights and, indeed, his income. In the economic order, there is strong protest against what is called "creeping socialism" which often includes in its condemnation social security legislation, rising income taxes, and federal aid to education. Not all who share this general lament of the rise of Leviathan include all of these things as of one piece, however, for some champion desegregation and condemn social security and *vice versa.*

If we are correct about Protestant ethics, the following principles define a Protestant approach to the problem.

First, we have no escape from facing the problem honestly, for Protestantism drives us into responsible citizenship. This means that we must try to be as informed as it is possible for us to be. The development of a strong state intervening in the economic order to a degree not approached prior to 1930 and in a way that is contrary to the *laissez-faire* theory of the state, has to be seen in the whole context of Western history as the counterpart in the United States of something which was happening elsewhere—in Germany, France, and Britain, for instance. Responsible citizenship includes an interpretation of history, hazardous and difficult as that interpretation always is.

Secondly, the Protestant understanding of man as creature and sinner, unable of himself to earn union with God, keeps us from identifying our judgments with the will of God. However much help we may get from the Church, from historians, from statesmen and from political parties, we have no final authorities save God and our own consciences, and God tells us that these two are not to be equated. Protestants should have a bond of community above their political differences in their common justification, their common awareness of their creatureliness and sin, and their resulting humility about their own political judgments and actions. In brief, Protestantism forbids idolatry; in this case, the deification of any political group, movement, or program. It de-religionizes the secular sphere, preventing it from giving rise to political crusades which turn religious, deifying themselves and satanizing their opponents. It prevents the ultimate self-righteousness of knowing that one is absolutely right.

This is a Protestant support for a democratic society. It permits deep differences to express themselves, and to seek to prevail without resorting to force before appeal has been made to the ballot-boxes or to the law courts of the land. It keeps deep differences from breaking the bond of community which we have in our common justification and in the community of the Spirit.

Thirdly, Protestant humility which comes of knowing our creatureliness and sin before God, does not paralyze us in regard to social action. We are commanded by God to live responsibly as both "sinners and justified" and we show forth our gratitude to God and our obedience to his command to love one another by our action. When Luther said that we must sin boldly, he meant that we must live with courageous responsibility yet not having the justification of the works of the law, that is, without being able to know that we are right. This courageous living will include the use of the coercive power of the state or even the use of revolutionary power against what we see as an unjust state, if there seems to us to be no alternative in the doing of the right as we see it.

Fourthly, since we can never claim to be absolutely right in our political, social, and economic judgments, we have always to criticize our programs in the light of the results which they produce. Protestantism produces or ought to produce a Christian pragmatism in matters of social policy and program which is responsive to its responsible critics and to experience. The will of God, for a Protestant, is learned on the anvil of historical experience insofar as specific political, economic, and social programs are concerned.

Fifthly, since we can never claim to be absolutely right in our political, social, and economic judgments, we must listen always and seriously to those who differ from us. Christians and non-Christians who are honest and sincere have a claim to our consideration both of their criticism of our own position and of their positive programs which differ from ours. This is the Protestant support of the democratic forum of public opinions. The churches themselves may play a great role here by providing the Christian context in which great issues may be debated. The churches do this without seeking a majority vote to find out the will of God, and certainly not to coerce a minority in any church into agreement with a majority. They do it in order to show the relevance of Christianity to social action; in order to subject major issues to corporate Christian scrutiny; in order to find for everyone's edification such consensus as does exist; in order to show each to the other such Christian responsibility, goodwill, and sincerity as may exist among those who embrace radically different political programs; in order that Christians may know the shock of sincere Christians differing deeply and thus be humbled in their own positions even when they cannot in conscience change them.

Whenever some consensus appears in meetings of Christians, this consensus may be set forth as a witness to the Christian conscience of others, although certainly not as a Christian "party line" with excommunication or church censure for those who disagree. Such a consensus appeared at the Ecumenical Conferences in 1937, in 1948, and in 1954.

Waldo Beach writes of the Oxford Conference on Life and Work in 1937:

In the area of economics the consensus report reflects some of the spirit of the Christian Socialist Movement in England and its American counterpart. Prevailing economic theory and practice, when measured by the yardstick of the Christian norm, is found universally wanting. In "free enterprise" capitalism, the Report recognizes the partial realization of Christian values; but on the debit side, it finds an exaltation of the profit motive over the sanctity of persons, tragic inequities in proportions of income, prevalent insecurity, and irresponsible concentrations of power. On the other hand, the communism offered as a cure-all for the capitalist ills the Report attacks as a delusive nostrum in its Utopianism, its materialism, and its disregard for the dignity of man as a free being responsible to God. Though it is not the role of the Church to specify one economic pattern as *the* Christian pattern, the Report does attempt to state main ethical norms (or "middle axioms") by which a mixed economy may balance the polar values of freedom and order.[1]

The Amsterdam Assembly of the World Council of Churches in 1948, according to the same author,

. . . reasserts its critical appraisal of both *laissez-faire* capitalism, the ideology of the West, and the nationalistic communism of Russia. It looks forward toward a responsible society whose spiritual constitution would transcend both of these alternatives and incorporate their truths . . .[2]

In the light of the foregoing, it may now be stated what one non-Roman Catholic, at least partially responsible to the classical Protestant tradition, sees as the immediate answer to the problem of "government initiative and private enterprise."

First, Christian love is an ultimate claim, capable of some realization in every historical situation, however distorted by sin that situation may be.

Secondly, part of the command to love is the demand of equality. "You shall love your neighbor *as yourself*" (Mk. 12:31), or even more stringently, "Therefore be imitators of God, as beloved children. And walk in love, as Christ loved us and gave himself up for us, a fragrant offering and sacrifice to God" (Eph. 5:1–2). Equality of treatment of our neighbor is the demand of love expressing itself

[1] Beach, Waldo, and Niebuhr, H. R., editors, *Christian Ethics—Sources of the Living Tradition,* copyright, Ronald Press Company, New York, 1955, pp. 486–487
[2] *Ibid.,* p. 488.

through the structure of justice in any human situation. Love transcends justice in self-sacrifice which offers itself to God for man in unity with Christ's perfect offering of himself to God for man. But love can never fall beneath justice in its struggle to achieve in and by the structures of society the highest approximation of equality which seems possible for the occasion.

Equality, however, is never simply rationalistic or mathematical equality which levels the more excellent down to the average. Justice gives every man his due and what each man's due is is something found out by the Christian conscience under the demands of love and justice, in the concrete situation. It cannot be found out simply by abstract deductive reason.

Thirdly, these norms of love and equality have to be applied in a world which already has realized much "equality before the law" and much "equality of opportunity" in some of its national traditions. The United States of America, for instance, is the sphere in which our question of government initiative and private enterprise poses itself for us. Love and justice fall upon us as demands, therefore, in an American context.

Fourthly, the crisis of the early thirties in our country was our form of the crisis which was felt earlier everywhere in Western or capitalist economy. There were multiple causes of that crisis but its marks were clear. There was uninvested capital with no incentive to invest and therefore to expand the productivity of the industrial order. There was a decline in the buying power of the masses of people directly related to mass unemployment and low incomes. There was a falling production index, increasing unemployment, and decreasing buying power. Government initiative met the depression with an American form of pump-priming which had its analogue everywhere in Western society. Government spending, government policing of methods of investment, government protection of labor's right to organize and bargain collectively, were not irresponsible driftings of government but considered undertakings by responsible men informed by the experience of other nations and with a conviction about the trends of Western economic life.

Fifthly, government spending for social services has been in part replaced and greatly supplemented since 1939 by government spending for war and for national defense. Our maintenance of a costly system of national defense simultaneously with an expanding consumer's economy is one of the most remarkable phenomena of human history, and greatly to the credit of both American government and American industry (including American organized labor), although it is primarily due to our favored place in history, our remarkable natural resources, and the momentum of our drive toward materialistic betterment.

At the moment our chief perils are inflation rather than depression, and use of raw materials, scientific knowledge, and industrial power for consumers' markets and profits, rather than for national defense.

Sixthly, no agency of human society can so well find out the proper balance between the demands of national defense and those of our consumer's market as can government; no other agency of human society can so well find out how to balance employment and just returns among our workers (agricultural, industrial, and white collar), the health of our industries (small and large), and of the geographical areas of the nation.

To say that no other agency of human society can do this so well, is not to say that government either does it well or will do it well. Government may and does call on the wisdom of all groups, but its task is to balance the claims of all special groups by using the composite wisdom of relatively disinterested groups.

Even more important than knowledge about the relatively just balancing of our economy in the light of our policies and ends is the fact that *only government can effect those balances*. Whatever natural balancing achievements may come from the play of a relatively free market, these achievements are now dependent upon government spending and government balancing of various claims on our economy.

Seventhly, government intervention in the economic order whether by direct ownership and operation of the means of production and of services, or by spending with some view to balancing the economy and its distributed fruits, or by policing the relationships of economic groups with their egocentric demands, inevitably increases government power and inevitably begins to unite political and economic power. These are the dangers of state socialism which ultimately cripples the creativity of private enterprise, produces apathy instead of the incentive to work in the general run of people, and bureaucracy and corruption in a government which increasingly combines political and economic power.

All of the Western nations, we less than all the other Western nations so far, have had to try to steer their course between the Scylla of a boom-bust unregulated economy and the Charybdis of a government planned economy that tends toward political and economic dictatorship. It is a difficult and dangerous course, although as Western history goes we have thus far stayed far away from the possibility of dictatorship. The decisions which come from such an analysis, insofar as the growth of the state's power and the problem of its intervention in the economic order are determinative, are generally in agreement with the directions which have been taken in American politics since 1932. I cannot believe that they are wholly wrong or that they were not—broadly speaking—necessary.

We may now turn to some of the other questions suggested for our discussion.

"The moral limits of the will to national survival" is one suggested subject. The phrasing correctly presupposes that there are moral limitations on a nation's will to survive. Unless there is an absolute moral imperative for every nation to survive under all circumstances—and that is not true—it would be immoral to remove the national will to survive from moral limits. What is asked for, then, is a casuistry which attempts to state the conditions under which a nation is morally obligated to sacrifice its national existence.

Protestant ethics, if we have properly understood it, will tell us only that the decision cannot be anticipated. Let us put the case in terms of our own national existence. If we distinguish nationality from the state, no problem of national survival is raised by a voluntary abridgment of state sovereignty or a total sacrifice of it—difficult to the point of impossibility as such action may be in actuality. Destruction of national existence can come in only two ways: 1) through mass demolition weapons or H-bomb war such as is pictured in Nevil Shute's novel, *On the Beach;* 2) through occupation by a foreign power or foreign powers that would in the course of time destroy everything which the nation embodies as a way of life. One could regard Communist invasion of the United States as likely to achieve this second kind of national destruction.

The national will to survive then, will express itself in resistance to a threat of total annihilation by overt war or in the refusal to surrender without condition or with conditions to powers rightly regarded as not to be trusted to honor a conditional surrender. Whatever may be the complexity of any actual decision and whatever may be the difficulties of applying the principles, the principles themselves, I think, are simple and clear. If the resistance to total annihilatory war with modern weapons clearly means total annihilation of the human race, then resistance could be undertaken by a Protestant Christian only under what he regarded as an absolute mandate of God. This, I believe, could be done. I could understand such a decision on the basis of "Give me liberty or give me death" and with the confidence that God not man says the final word. Despite the fact that I could understand and not condemn as un-Christian such a decision, I should oppose it with all my powers and stand for total and if necessary, unconditional, surrender. The basis of such a decision is simple. At this point—the point of certain annihilation of the human race—I should become an absolute pacifist on relativist grounds. The decision to end the human career on this planet I should have to abdicate. This hypothetical case, however, really does not fall under our topic, for the will to national survival would, if maintained under certainty of total human destruction, destroy the nation itself.

The tragic character of such a crisis toward which world history may well be moving lies in the fact that certainty of total annihilation of humanity may not be clear and certainly will be denied by many false prophets even if it is highly probable. If certainty of total destruction is not clear, then the decision has to be made on the basis of estimated probabilities and calculated risks. Any number of factors will enter such a decision. For instance, the decision of the United States not to defend itself against a Communist attack would leave the non-Communist nations without a defender that has sufficient national power to defend them. The United States would, therefore, be a bearer of a righteousness not its own and of a will-to-survive not wholly nation-centered. The decision would then have to be made morally on the basis of choosing the lesser of two evils. On the whole, given the conviction that resistance is the lesser of two evils I believe the Protestant ethic of remaining responsible rather than abdicating responsibility would tend to resistance to the point of taking a calculated risk of eliminating mankind. Protestant responsibility which remains responsible even as it is involved in increasing evil, is a very dangerous moral principle. This does not mean that it is immoral.

Protestant responsibility which incurs the risk of being wrong and remains responsible for choosing the least of evils may be illustrated in terms of a typical case. A pregnant wife and her family which is composed of a husband and five young children is told by competent medical authorities after consultation, that without a direct surgical abortion there is a very high probability that she and her unborn child will die. Some Protestants will regard this situation as one in which the wife in consultation with the husband may make a decision which incurs the risk of being wrong as to the medical facts (the high probability of both mother and child dying) and may choose what seems to her the lesser of two evils, the saving of the life of the mother at the expense of the life of the unborn child. It is not clear to them that a decision to risk the birth is the only Christian decision. It is, of course, quite clear that the refusal of a direct abortion is not contrary to Christian ethics.

The question of religious freedom for minority groups, particularly for nonreligious groups, is a question about the policy of a state since the state alone has the power to coerce religious education or church membership. Our question, therefore, lies in the area of church teaching about the Christian citizen's attitude and action in respect to his state's policy. History gives us no uniformly Protestant position in regard to this, although the modern democratic states have on the whole been supported overwhelmingly by Protestantism in their policies of absolute religious freedom to all minorities (or majorities, for that matter) including nonreligious or even missionary atheistic groups. It would not be inaccurate, it seems to me, to say that modern Protestantism favors a state which guarantees absolute religious freedom in regard to belief, choice or rejection of religious education, church affiliation and propagation of religious or antireligious views. The question is somewhat differently answered, however, where conduct classifying as moral is at issue. Congress in 1882 and in 1887 legislated to destroy Mormon polygamy and it is to be seriously doubted that religiously supported polygamy would be championed by any Protestants against state enforcement of our monogamous marriage laws. As a former Solicitor General of the United States, Charles Faby, has written: "Concededly, the free exercise of religion is not 'absolute,' as, for example, in the case of polygamy, breach of the peace, child labor, or refusal to bear arms." [3]

The reason that Protestantism as a whole complex movement has tended definitely to help create the modern state with its policy of freedom of religion, again lies in the Protestant understanding of God and man expressed in the doctrine of justification by faith. According to that understanding, God's final appeal to man lies in the love with which God loves us in His crucified Incarnate Son. The suasiveness of the Cross is God's final summons to man. For church or state to try to coerce belief is a negation of God revealed in Christ. At great cost to Himself God gives freedom to man and respects that freedom absolutely to the depth point of the Cross. The other side of justification-by-faith theology's support of freedom of religion lies in the nature of faith itself. Faith is not faith if it is not voluntary and no man can finally have faith for another.

---

[3] *Religion, Education and the Supreme Court* in Law and Contemporary Problems, Religion and the State issue, Vol. 14, No. 1, School of Law, Duke University, Winter 1949.

Furthermore, coercion of any kind is repugnant to a Christian, for it treats a human being as a thing, an object, dehumanizing him. Coercion is, therefore, a last resort for all Christians and only to be used when it is necessary to maintain order, to execute justice or to prevent injustice.

Unfortunately this is far from solving all of the problems which cluster around the subject of religious freedom. Everything that we have said about religion being voluntarily accepted can also be said about education. Yet it seems to be clear to an overwhelming majority of the citizens of our forty-eight States that compulsory education is good for the young up to a certain age.

Several things seem to be true here.

1) Most of us, perhaps all of us, to some degree, need an element of compulsion from outside of us to help us do what we know is good for us.

2) Immature persons need some element of external compulsion to expose them to things which are good for them.

3) Sheer compulsion can create an absolute rebellion on the part of those who are compelled which prohibits any internal and voluntary acceptance of that which is thrust upon them, however good for them it may be.

4) Compulsion therefore plays its proper role when it helps us do that which we know we ought to do or when it guarantees for us an exposure to that which by its own truth will attract us.

Because of these factors, the ultimate principle of freedom of religion by no means solves all of the problems. Is a man really free religiously when he is free to reject a religious outlook which he has never understood?

To the Roman Catholic and to the Protestant, Christianity is even more necessary to human fulness of living than human language. No one refuses to teach language to children until they are mature enough to choose which language they desire to speak. At least one language is necessary for them before they can understand another language and choose to speak it. So also he who experiences no religion is not capable of choosing among several religions. Consideration of such facts helps us to understand why, despite Protestantism's general championship of the modern state's development toward absolute freedom of religion, there are many problems of application of this principle about which there are sincere disagreements within Protestant denominations.

The First Amendment of our United States' Constitution prohibits Congress from making laws "respecting an establishment of religion, or prohibiting the free exercise thereof" and the Fourteenth Amendment prohibits any State from doing likewise. A host of Supreme Court decisions have applied these constitutional principles to various problems. Perhaps the most controversial of these decisions is the McCollum v. Board of Education of Champaign County, Illinois, which seemed to outlaw all teaching of religion in ways that involve the public schools.

Protestantism in the United States seems to have clear agreement on the principle that freedom of religion, as defined by the Constitution shall be guaranteed to our citizens by our government which is, of course, responsible also for the interpretation and application of the principle to our national life. But Protestants as citizens may and do disagree as to the rightness of some of those interpretations and applications and urge as citizens the acceptance by the state of their views.

We turn now to the Protestant ethics of marriage, divorce, remarriage after divorce, sexual morality, and planned parenthood.

All Christendom is agreed on one level, the highest level, the Christian ethic of marriage. The divine purpose in the sexual differentiation of human beings is indissoluble monogamous marriage. This is a purpose written deeply into the nature of man himself; it is a part of the Natural Law or, as some Protestants would prefer to say, it is a part of the Order of Creation. It is also what Roman Catholics and others call Divine Positive Law, that is, a revealed command of God. One of the several Scriptural grounds for this view is in St. Mark's Gospel, Chap. 10:2–12:

> And the Pharisees came to him, and asked him, Is it lawful for a man to put away his wife? tempting him.
>
> And he answered and said unto them, What did Moses command you?

And they said, Moses suffered to write a bill of divorcement, and to put her away.

And Jesus answered and said unto them, For the hardness of your heart he wrote you this precept.

But from the beginning of the creation God made them male and female.

For this cause shall a man leave his father and mother, and cleave to his wife;

And they twain shall be one flesh: so then they are no more twain, but one flesh.

What therefore God hath joined together, let not man put asunder.

And in the house his disciples asked him again of the same matter.

And he saith unto them, Whosoever shall put away his wife, and marry another, committeth adultery against her.

And if a woman shall put away her husband, and be married to another, she committeth adultery.

The most apparent difference between Roman Catholic ethics on marriage and Protestantism lies in the Protestant belief that marriage may be dissolved by other facts than the death of one of the parties and that remarriage can take place. Luther, for instance, held adultery and desertion to be grounds for divorce. ("Divorce" is used here in sense of a dissolution of marriage making each party eligible for marriage to another. "Separation from bed and board" leaves no possibility of marriage except with the original partner. Annulment, of course, means that there was no marriage to begin with.) [4]

Each Protestant communion defines the conditions under which it will solemnize the second marriage of a divorced person and fixes the authority which may make such a decision. It would be generally accurate to say, I believe, that most Protestant bodies give the local pastor the responsibility for such a decision and that few requests for remarriage after divorce are denied where there are no other complicating moral problems.

Beneath this seeming laxness of discipline in Protestantism we

[4] The Eastern Church takes the same position in principle as Western Catholicism but regards some marriages as dissolved by a spiritual death.

may see the still powerful influence of the classical Protestant doctrine of justification by faith alone. There is, of course, also much that is due to the new attitudes which have arisen as the result of secular equalitarianism and its doctrine of maximum freedom for the individual. Protestantism's general non-authoritarianism is, in part, a development of its original affirmation that ecclesiastical authority may not be identified with the authority of God. It is also, in part, a general reception of the modern democratic spirit which fixes responsibility for actions on the individual person as far as is possible.

Protestantism has written very little casuistry since the seventeenth century and its general lack of casuistry is expressed in its lack of casuistry in regard to the special *case,* remarriage after divorce. On the whole, Protestantism manifests a very strong and clear tendency to hold that the church is not authorized by God to dictate specific moral decisions to its members. Rather, the church proclaims the Gospel, administers the Sacraments, worships God, and instructs the membership in Christian ethical principles, leaving the individual person with the responsibility for moral decisions in specific situations. This might be called an attitude of "Love God and do as you please" which is far from libertine, if it is properly understood. Protestantism, therefore, has the virtue of recognizing the unique aspects of every human situation which cannot be grasped beforehand by casuistical thought. In Catholic language, Protestantism is a tremendous emphasis upon the cardinal virtue of prudence, that is, the informed Christian conscience making moral judgments which apply to unique cases the principles of Christian ethics. There is no necessary reason why Protestantism may not return to the production of casuistry, but, if it remains true to itself, Protestant churches will use whatever casuistry they develop for the education and illumination of the individual's conscience and will not legislate casuistry in the form of ecclesiastical canons.

In respect to the ethic of marriage, the deepest difference between Protestantism and Roman Catholicism lies in Protestantism's attitude to sexual intercourse and its meaning and purpose. From the standpoint of Protestantism, both medieval and modern Western Catholicism has been pulled away from the Biblical understanding of sexuality and sexual intercourse by pagan mystical and ascetic influences. Protestantism abolished celibacy as a Christian way of life higher than that of the married estate. Luther prepared the way for a new attitude to sex which has been steadily developing within Protestantism since the Reformation, but which has achieved full articulation only in the twentieth century.

This relatively new view has been well put by Derrick Sherwin Bailey, an Anglican, as follows:

Since it is as a sexual union established and sustained by sexual intercourse that marriage is distinguished from every other kind of legitimate relation or partnership between man and woman, the purpose of sex must inevitably determine to no small extent the purpose of marriage itself. It must not be overlooked, therefore, that sexual intercourse, whether or not it results in conception, always has profound consequence, in the realm of personal relation. The "one flesh" *henosis* is not merely a by-product of a biological function. Marriage derives its ontological meaning, not from the procreative capacity of husband and wife, but from the sexual love by which they are united in a special and significant personal relation. Intercourse may imply the possibility of procreation, but it means the certainty of union in "one flesh."

May we say, then, that marriage has different, rather than primary and secondary, ends?—that its chief institutional (and biological) purpose is procreation; that in relation to the personal life its first object is integration and fulfillment; and that ontologically its unitive end is primary.

But he finds even this unsatisfactory and argues further:

In regard to its ends, as in other respects, marriage must be assessed primarily as a personal relation, and with reference to its ontological character—and this leads inevitably to the conclusion (which Scripture supports) that its principal purpose is unitive. It must be made clear that this does not imply any minimizing of the importance of procreation, although it cannot any longer be accepted as the chief end of marriage. The purpose of the foregoing reconsideration has been to show that the first purpose for which God calls men and women together (in marriage) is that they may become one flesh; it has not been to depreciate the first cause "for which matrimony was ordained." The unitive end of marriage takes precedence over the procreative end simply because it stands in a closer relation than the latter to the essential nature of the *henosis,* and since it does so by virtue of Divine ordination, no contravention of any principle of natural law is involved.[5]

Emil Brunner in *The Divine Imperative* puts the principle tersely:

. . . the Christian ethic must stand for the independent meaning of the erotic and sex element within marriage as an expression of love, not merely as a means of procreation (p. 368).

The implications of this are obvious. While sexual intercourse as the expression of marital love is in no way divorced from the purpose of procreation and the marriage is in no sense freed from the responsibility of parenthood, every particular act of sexual intercourse is not directly identified with the procreative end of sexual intercourse. Planned parenthood, therefore, may become a possibility without contravening either divine or natural law. For many Protestants planned parenthood has become even more than this, it has become a Christian ethical demand.

R. Paul Ramsey, Professor of Religion at Princeton University, has written:

The Catholic view is not so much read from nature as out of the weight of the tradition of asceticism which places a premium on continence, whether the continence of "the religious" or general continence adopted for grave reason within marriage or the periodic continence of the rhythm method. By contrast, Protestant teaching is that, in face of perils to the mother in having more children, there is a right and a positive duty to continue the mutual nurturing of marital love through intercourse which employs contraceptives. This is within the law of nature or among the things to do or not to do which arise simply from reflection upon the nature of man, no other considerations of fact being taken into account. Then, in the light of the social consequences of the world's mounting population, there may also be a positive duty to use contraceptives for the limitation and planning of parenthood (not its avoidance). This might be called the *jus gentium,* which arises from reflection

[5] *The Mystery of Love and Marriage,* Harper & Brothers, New York, 1952, pp. 107–108.

upon the nature of man as man, namely, the transcendence of the personal, this time taking into account other factual considerations.[6] Such teaching is also Biblical, for the Bible places the constitutive essence of marriage in the "unity of flesh" between man and wife, and in the cure of Adam's loneliness, even while with all the other creatures they are commanded to be fruitful and multiply.[7]

Let us be clear at the end of this discussion of marriage and sex that this new Protestant view of sex is still within the framework of the New Testament and Christian ethic of monogamous marriage. It teaches that sexual intercourse by divine ordering and, therefore, by its intrinsic nature, belongs only within the order of monogamous marriage.

This trend in Protestantism does not accept the Roman Catholic position that absolute continence or periodic continence which uses the so-called rhythm method are the only permissible methods of planned parenthood. It sees no final distinction between man's responsible use of mechanical or chemical contraception and his use of the periods of infertility in the biological cycle of the woman's life.

There is no Protestant consensus on the difficult problems of artificial insemination but at the present time, it seems accurate to say that Protestant moral opinion is overwhelming against artificial insemination where the husband is not the donor, and sees no objection to it where the husband is the donor, whatever procedures may be involved.

[6] *Cf.* Jacques Maritain's definitions of *jus naturale* and *jus gentium* in *The Rights of Man and Natural Law*, C. Scribner's Sons, New York, 1943, pp. 68–69.

[7] *New York University Law Review*, Vol. 31, No. 7, November, 1956, pp. 1194–1195.

IV

THE ETHICAL CULTURE MOVEMENT

BY

JEROME NATHANSON

*Administrative Leader, The New York Society
for Ethical Culture*

No one can speak "authoritatively" for the Ethical Culture Movement. This is because respect for differences and for individuality is central to our position. Yet in what follows, while I speak personally, I am also expressing what is a substantially shared point of view.

Dogmatism to my mind has no place in ethics, either in theory or in practice. If an ethical judgment cannot be rationally or experimentally vindicated, then it should be changed to one that can be. While the life of reason rejects dogmatism, however, it does depend upon generalization or, speaking technically, upon universal propositions. In just the same way, ethics consists of universals or it is nothing at all. The sometimes agonizing difficulty of trying to reach ethical decisions lies in the problem of determining the relationship of a universal to a specific situation.

There is something arbitrary about defining terms in any complex subject-matter. "Ethics" and "morality" are often used interchangeably, and this is justified etymologically. Yet I distinguish between them because, for me, it helps to clarify certain other distinctions I think important. "Morality" I identify with the *mores,* the customs, of any given group of people; it is therefore necessarily relative to the given cultural milieu. "Ethics" I identify with generalizations about the relationships which ought to prevail among human beings; and insofar as such generalizations are valid, they have to be applicable to any and all moral systems.

Generalization in ethics, if it is to have any validity, must be generalization from experience. This brings us to one of the touchier questions in contemporary discussion. It is widely held that facts are one thing and values, including ethical values, quite another. This position has more than a surface plausibility to it. But I do not believe that facts and values are in two separate compartments or on two different levels of thinking, discourse, or living. A so-called ethical end which is not within the scope of human potentialities is not an ethical end at all. Insofar as it is beyond human reach, such an end, instead of being ethical, would rather be punitive or sadistic or masochistic, depending upon who was setting it up for whom, and for what purpose. In other words, what *ought* to be is inescapably involved with what *is*. If it is not inescapably involved with the facts of life, then it ought not to be. To enjoin a businessman to behave in a way that would put him out of business, for example, is not to make of him an ethical businessman. It is to make of him no businessman at all! The basic conditions of functioning vocationally, the facts of a business culture, are an essential part of what is involved in trying to conduct one's business life ethically. It is true that facts do not determine values, that what is cannot be the determinant of what ought to be. It is also true that reflection upon facts, in the light of human experience and aspiration, does determine values.

All such reflection requires a criterion, a point of departure. This is what raises the basic question of sanctions. From the viewpoint of Ethical Culture, what sanctions are there for whatever we mean by an ethical pattern of life? In answering this question, I should make clear that I am not discussing the religious character of the Ethical Culture Movement. This is another question. I do not believe that either ethical religion or any other religion is indispensable to ethics.

This takes us back to the matter of dogmatism. "Dogmatism" I take to be the positive, unqualified assertion of the truth of a proposition which cannot rationally or experimentally be shown to be valid. To assert that the one and only aim of the human enterprise is the glorification of God is an example of dogmatism. This proposition may or may not be true. The point is that, on objective grounds, none of us can either know or prove that it is or is not true.

Let us look at the same matter from a different point of view. The proposition that one plus one equals two is not an example of dogmatism. It is rather a postulate in a system of mathematics. One might just as well postulate that one plus one equals three. In a mathematical system, or any system that can be pursued logically, the postulate is what determines what follows rationally. Any given postulate cannot get its vindication or justification within the system for which it is the point of departure. It can be justified, if at all, only in some other system. In Euclidean geometry the postulate or axiom that two parallel lines extended indefinitely will never meet is an essential part of that system; it is taken for granted, although its truth cannot be demonstrated within the system. Many centuries after Euclid, another mathematician asked himself what would follow if one reversed the postulate. Supposing one were to assume that two parallel lines extended indefinitely would meet. What then would follow? Thus non-Euclidean geometry was discovered, with all its vast implications for the development of modern physics.

The nature of postulates in a mathematical system has bearing on universal propositions in ethics. They are not to be taken dogmatically. Neither are they demonstrable within a given ethical system. Whatever validity they have is derived from other areas of human experience and reflection or, more importantly, from the consequences of their acceptance. The validity of an ethical universal is to be determined by the consequences to which it leads. Nor is this view narrowly pragmatic in the sense in which "pragmatism" denotes a certain way of philosophizing. It is compatible with a wide spectrum of philosophic beliefs.

Let me now turn more specifically to what I mean by ethics and religion, in order to make clear what I have in mind in saying that they are not mutually indispensable. By "ethics" I mean the principle or principles of right *living*. The emphasis is made to distinguish my position from that of those ethical philosophers who regard ethics as simply an analysis of propositions containing the predicates "good" or "right." Nor do I think that ethics is simply a matter of preference or of taste. This is what leads to the chaos of ethical relativism: if the Nazis' standard of conduct differs from ours, nevertheless they must do what they think to be right, just because they regard it as right.

The point I am making is illustrated by a story told of the late philosopher Morris Raphael Cohen. While lecturing to a class in the City College of New York some years ago, Professor Cohen was increasingly annoyed by a young man seated in the back of the room who kept waving his hand excitedly in order to attract attention. Finally, when he could ignore the youngster no longer, he resignedly asked what it was he wanted to say. The student remarked, "Professor Cohen, you have just said that this and this is the case, but from my point of view the reverse is true." Professor Cohen pierced him with a look and retorted, "From your point of view, young man, you're right. The trouble is that your point of view is wrong!"

Neither do we in Ethical Culture believe that ethics is basically emotive, that to say something is "good" is simply to have a good feeling about it. Nor do we accept the positivistic position, that whatever one can meaningfully call "right" or "good" is simply what different people have as a matter of fact designated by these terms. When we speak of ethics we mean a principle or principles having to do with the essential business of life as it is lived in day-by-day human relationships.

This sense of ethical living does not have anything necessarily to do with religion. The distinction is one of the utmost practical importance. Just as there are persons who are color-blind and some who are tone-deaf, so there are those who have no religious sensitivity or, at least to take them at the level of their own acknowledgment, no awareness of any special religious need. No matter how few or many such persons there may be, they are not to be ignored. Yet ethics is not to be considered any less important to them, or their ethics to the rest of us, just because they are not religious.

By "religion" I do not mean simply a relation to God or to the gods. For me—indeed, for the Ethical Culture Movement as a whole—agnostics, for example, can be and sometimes are genuinely religious people. By "religion" I mean rather a person's sense of relatedness to the totality of being, however he conceives that totality or whatever he regards it as being. To put it differently, religion is the effort to apprehend rationally, emotionally, or mystically, if you will, the place of the finite in the oceans of the infinite.

Felix Adler, the founder of the Ethical Culture Movement, based his religious view on the conception of a spiritual universe. While he expressed the hope that other people, especially future Leaders, would share this view, he insisted that he was in no sense attempting to lay down what other people should believe about this or other metaphysical or theological questions.

Speaking for myself, I believe that there is an infinite universe which in its totality is beyond anything that human experience will ever know. The infinite universe will always be larger than the experienced universe. How is one to plot this relationship? It is at this point in human thought and experience that Christianity has a special power. Jesus, the man, is a symbol of the finite; Christ, the second person of the Trinity, is the symbol of the infinite. Finite and infinite are thus joined in one personality. Logically and metaphysically this belief has at least great beauty, because it deals with the most critical of all human problems in a tremendously persuasive way.

Religion, in other words, is a sense of the whole of things, not really understood (who of us can understand it?) but as it somehow encompasses the human enterprise. Accordingly, while it is possible to be committed to ethical living without being religious, it is not possible to be religious without having that fact color every aspect of behavior, including the ethical. To use the logical terminology, it is an a-symmetrical relationship.

These considerations should throw light on what I meant earlier when I said that in discussing patterns of ethics as seen by the Ethical Culture Movement, I am not discussing our religious character. I think, to be sure, that human life would be vastly more barren without religion. The central point involved here, however, is its bearing on the question of sanctions for a given point of view. Because, while Ethical Culture believes in the universality of a basic ethical principle of life, it also believes in the impossibility of universalizing any one sanction or justification for this ethical universality, in the absence of objective proof about the rightness or wrongness of any one cosmic, theological or metaphysical view.

I will be more specific on the latter point. One person, for example, may regard prayer as an integral and indispensable part of what he thinks of as his spiritual life. To another person prayer is inconceivable. How is one to dogmatize about such matters? Who is to say whether the universe, either through a personal God or in some other way, is concerned with the moral and spiritual progress of individual human beings? For one person, human experience would be intolerable unless meaningful prayer is a fact of life. To a person at the other extreme, the idea that there should be a Supreme Being sensitive to one's needs or difficulties is completely unbelievable.

The Ethical Culture Movement, as a movement, takes no position on such questions. An actual incident may be helpful by way of illustration. At the time of the Allied invasion of North Africa during World War II, the first important engagement of American troops, President Roosevelt requested that there be special prayers in all religious institutions on the following Sabbath. I was presiding at the meeting at our New York City Meeting House on that Sunday, and at the conclusion called attention to the President's request. In doing so I said, "We in the Ethical Movement don't pray, but we shall have a moment of silence." Because people's emotions were so deeply engaged, the period of silence was a most meaningful shared experience. At the conclusion of the meeting a little old lady, who was a lifelong member of our Society and whose parents were among the founders of our Movement, came up to me and said, "I have a bone to pick with you. I understood you to say this morning that we in the Ethical Movement don't pray. I think you're wrong. Isn't what you meant to say, rather, that *as a Movement* we don't pray. How do you know whether I pray or not?" She was completely in the right. I had no way of knowing whether or not she prayed and, much more importantly, from the viewpoint of our Movement it was none of my business.

There are members of Ethical Culture to whom prayer is an indispensable dimension of human experience. For most of those who do pray, I suspect (though again I have no way of *knowing*) that they do not regard this as an appeal to a personal deity who will help in any given crisis, but rather as a statement of their innermost and highest aspirations. And, indeed, what *are* we to know about such things and how such things ultimately happen? Even John Dewey once remarked that the upshot of things is not with us, try as we will.

The essential point is that for Ethical Culture the attempt to live an ethical life is not regarded as being contingent upon the acceptance or rejection of any one over-belief, no matter what that over-belief may be. Our common ground, our basis for coming together, is a commitment to the effort to live ever more ethically. In an infinite universe there is room for a great many differing over-beliefs. For Ethical Culture, the only ones to be rejected are those which dogmatically assert themselves to the necessary exclusion of any differing views.

This does not mean that equal credibility is to be attached to any and all over-beliefs. There are some people who are obviously fools, and their over-beliefs may be plain foolish. But the basic ethical principle for us, to which I now come, is compatible with a great many different over-beliefs. This is why, from the viewpoint of Ethical Culture, the supreme irony of the Western religious tradition is the disputation and bloodshed which have come in the name of religion itself. Viewed objectively, there is no more reason why I should accept the views of others than that they should accept mine. When it comes to good works in the community at large, as a matter of fact, we all know that they are frequently of an interdenominational character, and embrace many people with no denominational affiliations whatever.

What, then, is the basic ethical principle from the viewpoint of Ethical Culture? Without trying to sound dogmatic, I shall express it succinctly. Felix Adler himself once put it in the most summary terms when he said that one should "so act as to elicit the best in another person and, thereby, in oneself." The "thereby" is the important word here. In the language of the tradition, one cannot save his soul alone. Neither is the ethical life advanced simply by being concerned with the well-being of other people. There is rather a mutuality, a reciprocal quality, an interrelationship. In logic, this proposition is stated as the principle of polarity. A helpful illustration is that of the blades of a pair of shears. They are not shears at all if there is only one blade. Both blades are necessary, coming at each other, in order to have a cutting edge. In human terms, persons as well must come to each other in order to have a growing or ethical edge. This is as true of the relations of groups as it is of those of individuals. Whatever is valid in the idea of cultural pluralism—one of the most important ideas in the world —stems from the principle that in the relations of group and group, people and people, race and race, emphasis upon the mutual promotion of distinctively fine things is what gives an ethical quality to the experience.

I have said that ethics means the application of universal principles to varying moral situations, morality in turn being relative to a given cultural milieu. Is it possible, for example, to live as ethically in a polygamous as in a monogamous culture? If so, what does this mean?

In an international students' seminar which I conducted a few years ago, a devout Moslem from Iraq was one day being guyed by a most sophisticated Egyptian Christian. The latter, tongue-in-cheek, remarked that while in theory a Moslem might have four wives, in practice he could have as many as he wanted and was able to maintain financially, because Moslem law makes divorce and remarriage so easy. The Moslem responded, in a gentle but moving voice: "It is true that the Koran says that a man may have four wives. But what else does it say? It says that he may have four wives if he loves each of them the same way and treats each of them accordingly. Mohammed himself knew that it is not possible for one to love and treat others identically. Therefore, no matter what the Koran allows in terms of the human situation, the really devout Moslem should have only one wife."

Now, regardless of this Moslem's sensitive demurrer, polygamy is still widely practiced and accepted. How is one to choose between it and monogamy on ethical grounds? If it could be demonstrated that a system of polygamy is more conducive to developing the best and finest potentials of human nature than a system of monogamy, then polygamy would be ethically superior. Under the guise of monogamy, to be sure, unless we are ready to close our eyes to the widespread and often enduring number of extra-marital relationships, actual polygamy is by no means exceptional in Western culture, as well. But in our culture, at the same time, tremendous numbers of us in all sincerity, and practically all of us at least nominally, believe in monogamy, because we believe it to be the best means of forwarding the best in interpersonal relationships.

Such matters, I repeat, are not subject to any absolute, *a priori* judgment. They are to be judged *a posteriori,* in terms of the consequences which follow from acting upon a given principle. Surely this does not imply the foolhardy suggestion that each of us or any of us should try to recapitulate the ethical thinking and struggles of mankind. There is the historical record of past consequences of past actions stemming from a variety of ethical principles; and these historical consequences are part and parcel of the data of our own endeavors. If we have judgment enough to do so, we profit from the knowledge and experience of the human race, from the reflections of the great thinkers and the prophetic insights of the great religious leaders. But the lessons of the past are fruitful only as they are approached in a non-dogmatic spirit.

To turn to physical science once more, a hypothesis gains in probability—it is never certain—as it is experimentally verified. After intense labors, primarily of a mathematical character, Einstein emerged with the now famous formula, E equals MC squared; that is, energy equals the mass of whatever is being considered times the speed of light squared. For some time this was a formula and nothing more, useful to theoretical physicists in their own speculations. But then there came the breakthrough in experimental physics, and nuclear energy emerged. From such experimental verification the formula received an extremely high degree of probability that it is indeed a valid generalization. I think that the case is no different when we consider ethics. Ethical principles are vindicated by the facts they create.

What is the relation of these general considerations to human nature? One side of the Western tradition has emphasized that man is essentially good. For did not God look upon His creation, including man, and call it good? There is the Roman Catholic modification, in its dogma of original sin, that while man is born essentially good he is also born with an inherent predisposition to evil. But on the other side, in some of the extreme wings of Protestantism, there is the belief that man is essentially evil, that he is a miserable and unworthy sinner who can be saved only by the mysterious intervention of God's grace.

Neither of these is the view of the Ethical Culture Movement. We believe that man is essentially neither good nor evil. We believe that he has vast potentials for both, and that the experience of reciprocal relationships is in a measure determinative of which qualities are to emerge. On this premise, no one need have been surprised at the emergence of almost unimaginable evil in our time, the bestiality in the relationships of some men to others. But neither should one be surprised at the emergence of a Gandhi or a Schweitzer. The great plasticity of human nature is what we regard as the essential datum of human life.

In saying that the nature of reciprocal relationships is a determinant of what qualities are to be manifested by people, we are brought to a consideration of the role of frustration in human experience. Life being what it is, there are necessary limitations to what we are and what we achieve. In the words that William James was so fond of quoting from Benjamin Blood, life is an "ever not quite"; or, in Browning's language, "Ah, but a man's reach should exceed his grasp, or what's a heaven for?" No matter what our sensitivities and aspirations, no matter how devotedly we try to sense the desirable relationship with another person and effectuate it, there are always the inadequacies that mark even the best of us. There is the pain, the suffering, the heartache of experience. The evil that I would not, that I do. Now central to us as we concentrate on the quality of reciprocal relationships is the idea that frustration itself, of whatever character, should never be regarded merely as a limitation. On the contrary, it is to be seen as an indispensable condition of one's own ethical growth. The manner in which one comes to terms with inadequacy and suffering has much to do with the effort to become more nearly adequate ethically.

Equally important in shaping the nature of reciprocal relationships is the degree and quality of an individual's participation in the social problems of his time and place. It is not as if an individual could become ethical on his own, and then bring his ethical attributes to bear on whatever social problems concern him. We believe the reverse is true. We believe that in trying to work with all kinds of people, of different backgrounds and attitudes, in behalf of common and justifiable aims, the ethical by-product for the self is an indispensable dimension of one's own development.

Ethical Culture, in the light of these beliefs, is as hospitable to the insights and contributions of depth psychology as it is to those of the physical sciences. For since we cannot be *certain* of the validity or truth of any ethical judgment, the more knowledge we have, the more dependable our judgments are likely to be.

Does this mean, then, a return to the Socratic dictum that knowledge is virtue? In a sense it does. But in saying this, let us remind ourselves that the Greek term is *areté* which, while frequently translated as "virtue," accurately means "excellence."

In returning to the Socratic dictum, however, we cannot do so in a naive or obvious sense. Nothing is more of a commonplace about human behavior than the frequency with which we do what we know is wrong (perhaps having an uneasy conscience in the process) or fail to do what we know to be right. This is a point at which we can get help from the insights of modern psychodynamics, where contemporary knowledge has helped us to return to Socrates from a more sophisticated point of view.

What so often stands in the way of our doing what we know to be right is either immaturity or emotional disturbance, whether of a neurotic or a psychotic character. This is not to say, as so many thinkers nowadays do in effect, that "ethics" is simply a poor word for "maturity." We must not be guilty of the fallacy of reducing ethics to psychology. A mature person may do what he thinks is right while having a wrong notion of what is right. I am not one who believes that Fascists or Nazis or Communists are necessarily immature people. Neither do I believe that all criminals are, by definition, sick people. There is a distinction. But maturity or, better, maturing is an essential condition of being able to live ever more ethically; of the never-ending struggle to get better knowledge of what is right; and of putting that knowledge to work.

This is not to say that "knowledge" is "certainty," nor is it to affirm that man is a rational being. I know that if I drive my car over a cliff, for example, it will crash. In saying that I know this will happen I am saying more than that I suspect it will or have reason for believing that it will happen. I mean that the odds are some billions to one that it will crash under these circumstances. By some fortunate chance, the car may not crash at all. One cannot be certain. But when things are characterized by such a high degree of probability, then we are right in regarding them as not simply belief but as knowledge.

Nor do ethics and ethical judgment rest on the belief that man is a rational being. Fortunately or not, the springs of human behavior are not rational. The problem is to take the springs of human behavior and their consequences and insofar as possible to organize them ever more rationally.

The compulsive behavior pattern of so many individuals is an illustration of this. Most of us should know by now, surely, that one of the worst things you can do with an alcoholic is to make hortatory appeals to him to stop drinking. He usually knows his fault and what it is doing to him even better than others do. He just cannot help himself, and the hortatory approach only makes him more miserable; and the greater the misery the greater the need to go on drinking. Such a person can be helped only if he genuinely wants to be helped. If he goes to a doctor, not because he wants to, but in order to satisfy someone else, then the doctor can do him no good. Yet there is a faith about human nature which has a great deal of vindication in experience. Sometimes, somehow, in differing ways, alcoholics as well as narcotic addicts and other victims of compulsion can be reached so that they will achieve a self-motivation for the necessary help. If this were not the case, no such person would ever be helped, whereas we know as a matter of fact that vast numbers of them have been and are now being helped. When Aristotle long ago said that man is the rational animal he did not mean that all men behave rationally or even that any man behaves rationally all the time. He meant that under certain circumstances it is possible for man to achieve rational patterns of behavior.

Maturity is freedom from the compulsions, of whatever character, which stand in the way of our behaving with reasonableness, with intelligence. Knowing what is right insofar as it is given to us to know, we are then, if sufficiently mature, at least able in a measure to do what we know. It is in this sense that we can affirm with reasonable confidence that knowledge is virtue.

How does one achieve maturity? It is a sobering thought that very few, if any, persons ever become completely mature. Maturity is a relative concept. It is relative to ourselves and our own potentials: here it is a question of integrity—not integrity in the sense simply of honesty, but of the integration, the unifying, the wholeness of personality. Maturity is also relative to the standards of the culture in which we live. If there is infantilism in the culture, as there is in so much of American entertainment, this has bearing both on our judgment of maturity and on our ability to achieve it.

Maturity is achieved through the *taking* of responsibilities. A person cannot have responsibility thrust upon him, even though the situation in which he finds himself may demand it. From an ethical point of view, one either takes the responsibility on himself, or it has no ethical bearing. Obviously, this means an inner discipline as against an outer or imposed discipline. Insofar as one can help a child develop an ethical personality, it can be done only by helping that child to take the responsibilities which characterize desirable reciprocal relationships.

The corollary of these considerations is that personality, or self-hood, is not given to us. We are not born as persons. We are born biologically, even though the smallest of infants will quickly manifest distinctively inherited characteristics. The achievement of self-hood is actually the creation of selfhood. This is why the idea of self-fulfilment, when set up as an ethical end, has always seemed fallacious to me. Taken literally, it would mean that there is a self somehow to be fulfilled. But, on the contrary, there is a self to be real-ized. The potentials are there but they must be actualized, and that is the nature of the creation of selfhood. Insofar as the potentials of the best and finest things in a person are thus realized, it is the creation of an ethical personality.

Yet there must be two simultaneous phases, of equal importance, in this creative process: self-acceptance and self-transcendence. The creation of ethical personality is contingent on self-acceptance. I think it impossible to achieve a healthful, ethical personality by constantly berating oneself with a sense of being a miserable sinner. This does not mean that one should not feel guilt as a dimension of one's own failure in responsibility. But it is to say that one ought not to regard himself as essentially a despicable being.

Now the reality of guilt is not to be confused with what we nowadays call the "sense of guilt." A great many people feel leeply guilty although there is no objective ground for guilt in heir present reality. Their feeling of guilt, for example, may be grounded in emotional conflicts of early childhood. On the other hand, there are a great many people who ought to feel guilty, because they do so much that is wrong, and yet have no sense of guilt at all. This is the paradox and the difficulty. The ethical life of mankind would indeed be advanced immeasurably if there were some conceivable way of assuring that those who are really guilty of wrongdoing could be made to feel their guilt, and to do something constructive about it.

However things may go in the latter respect, an attitude of self-acceptance is a condition of ethical growth. Yet there is a precariousness about this, for the whole matter is so intimately related to a person's earliest experiences as a child in his family. In no small degree, an attitude of self-acceptance is contingent upon an early experience in the family that the child is wanted for himself alone. This experience is at the core of a child's development toward self-acceptance, and this is the nub of the issue of planned parenthood, to which I shall return.

The other major phase in the creation of ethical personality is self-transcendence. What we are at any given time is never good enough. We ought always to be striving to become more nearly adequate than we now are. We must be endeavoring constantly to pass beyond, to transcend, where we are now.

It is this tension in the personality—the dialectic relationship between self-acceptance and self-transcendence—which is the central dynamics of ethical development.

One other general consideration before dealing with specific issues. This is the role of punishment in its relationship to an ethical life. Not all of my colleagues in the Ethical Culture Movement agree with me about this. But I think that punishment is ethically justified, with adults as well as with children, when it has educative intent and import. When wrong is done, when a personality has become grooved in antisocial behavior, and that behavior is not dictated by compulsive but by misdirected ideas, then punishment plays a desirable role with respect to desirable reciprocal relations.

As against the belief that is so commonly held, the late Dr. James S. Plant, one of the ablest of child psychiatrists, used to observe that from a psychological point of view it is not necessarily bad for a child to be punished, even physically, by a parent. He used to insist that what is bad for the child's development is to say to the child, "If you do so and so, then this and this will happen to you," and not to have it happen. A stable body of expectations is essential for a child in building up his sense of health as a personality and his sense of acceptance by others. A child will frequently go after an adult, particularly a parent, almost to the point of the expiration of patience, just to determine when he will be told that this is enough, and anything more will lead to punishment. This is, in the terminology we have just been using, part of the tension between self-acceptance and self-transcendence for the child, who needs to be told as precisely as possible what the limits are for his behavior.

Dr. Milton Sapirstein, the psychoanalyst, has written a searching analysis of what he calls "the paradox of the screaming mother." In it he raises a double-barrelled question. First, he asks how it is that so many children of relatively serene parents, who never raise their voices in the household and never punish their children, raise children who turn out to be neurotic. Second, he points to those busy housewives whose children on occasion pester them beyond endurance who, having exploded with impatience, then calm down; such mothers frequently raise children who are much healthier emotionally than the children of the others. The paradox is resolved, again, in the context of that sense of limits to tolerable behavior which is related to the dynamics of personality tension.

Punishment, I repeat, is ethically justified when it has this educative dimension to it. It is completely unjustified when it does not have this dimension to it. As a not unimportant aside: if any form of punishment is completely unjustified and completely wrong ethically, I think capital punishment is it. To call it "punish-

nent" at all is in itself a supreme irony. For since it surely cannot be punitive in the sense of being educative for the person who
is victimized, it is essentially, however we may gloss the fact over,
either retributive or revengeful.

Let us turn now to some of the specific issues of ethical concern
which have been raised for this series of discussions. I have written
most sketchily about my sense of the relationship between the
maturing process and an ethical life. Despite the sketchiness, I
hope some of the import of what I have in mind will become
clearer in the context of my view of the marriage relationship.
For I regard marriage as *the* maturing relation in life. To put
the matter differently and I hope not too paradoxically: it is my
belief that most people, at the age when young people ordinarily
marry, are not mature enough to be married.

This lack of sufficient maturity for marriage is, if anything,
fostered by our instruments of mass communication: the soap
operas on radio and television, the cheap romantic fiction, the
infantilism of so many movies. Young people are accordingly encouraged in the romanticism that when a beautiful girl or a handsome young man (meaning, projectively, oneself!) meets the
properly attractive person of the other sex, love and marriage
follow and that is all there is to it. Then they discover that this is
by no means all there is to it. And, having been so ill-prepared for
the marital "facts of life," they dissolve that marriage and walk
into another—perhaps on and on—in the endless pursuit of a
chimera.

The basic point for me, involving both the ideas of maturity and
of frustration, is this. All marriages (unless they are between
those rare people who are the equivalent of saints) will be marked
by periods of tension and frustration. We have already observed
that coming to terms with frustration and transcending it is part
of one's development as an ethical personality. Instead of tension
and frustration in a marriage becoming the occasion for dissolving
it, as is so frequently the case, they ought to be seen rather as the
basic ethical challenge to the two people involved. It is this that

ought to help them mature as ethical personalities. For the attempt to transcend these very frustrations is, in the vernacular, the effort to "grow up" enough to be married. If one were obliged to give any one ethical meaning to the marriage relation, I would say that these challenges to maturing are it.

Aside from this matter of maturing, I do not believe that the question of the meaning of marriage is a meaningful one. The aim of marriage is simply the realization of whatever is deepest and best in the life aspirations of the couple married, whatever those aspirations may be. Or, to put it differently, the aim of marriage should not be for the husband to try to make the wife more like himself, or for the wife to try to make the husband more like herself. The ethical concern in marriage ought to be to stimulate the very distinctive things in both parties to the relationship which can be educed in the process of the intimate involvement of two people's lives.

It is in this context that the question of intermarriage must be seen. Over the years I have officiated at the marriages of a great many people of different religious backgrounds. I stress the matter of background, because when a genuine religious difference exists between people at the time when they are contemplating marriage, then quite another question presents itself. Granted that periods of tension come in most marriages, to add the tension of religious difference, particularly as it may focus on the religious upbringing of children, is to invite trouble. I have sometimes refused to officiate at a marriage under these circumstances when I have had reason to believe that the couple involved have not tried with sufficient maturity to come to terms with this reality.

But the question of intermarriage is to my mind not a question of ethical principle. It is rather a question of prudence or of judgment. For when people of different backgrounds come out to very much the same general attitude toward life, then the ethical principle of maturing through the reciprocal stimulation of the distinctive best applies here as it does in any other marriage. In my experience as a matter of fact, when two people of different backgrounds have reached the same general point of view toward life, the marriage may be even more enriching than others, just because of the different religious and cultural sensitivities they bring to the relationship.

When intermarriage involves people of different ethnic, instead of simply religious, backgrounds, it is quite a different matter. Here the pressure of community attitudes becomes of far greater importance. This can be seen in the fact that intermarriage between a white person and a Negro, or a white person and an Asian, is much simpler in France, for example, than it is in the United States, because of the far greater degree of toleration and acceptance of individual choice when it comes to matters of intimate personal life. Even in the United States, it is simpler in such a metropolitan center as New York than it is in a small community. For in a metropolitan center, no matter how "different" you may be, or how much off the beaten path your pattern of life, you can usually find a number of other people who think and behave as you do. Still, in this country, one does not have to go to the small towns or the rural regions to learn how much the general community attitude is strictly set against intermarriage of an interracial character. Nevertheless I think that this, as ought to be true of all other intimate personal relationships, is a private matter. Neither legislatively nor in any other way should the community dictate to people what they ought to do about such concerns. This is a respect for personality which all persons are owed by the community in which they live. That this is frequently not what actually happens does not change the consideration that it is what ought to happen.

This has special bearing with respect to children. Just because children of such a marriage are more likely than not to learn very early in life that they are somehow "different" from other children, it is essential that parents be able to give them from the start a deep and abiding sense of inner security. This requires, therefore, a greater maturity at the time of marriage itself than is otherwise the case.

Since I have already stressed what I regard as the essentially private character of a marital relationship, it ought to be evident that this holds with respect to sexual aspects of marriage, as well. Contraception and planned parenthood have to be seen in this light. How a man and wife behave sexually, as long as they treat each other with respect, is their own business and not the business of anyone else.

Accordingly, I approach the problem of planned parenthood not from the point of view of the parent but of the child. Just as there is no greater blessing in the world than for a child to be deeply wanted by parents when he is born, so there is no greater curse than to be born to parents who do not really want the child. Heaven only knows how many neurotic adults in our culture today, people causing endless trouble to themselves and others, are what they are now because they were rejected children when they were born; and they are simply taking out, one way or another, all the resentments, not against the parents, but their surrogates in society generally. No parent has the ethical right to bring a child unwanted into the world. Not only do I regard contraception as ethically justified, therefore, but as an essential of ethical family living.

The problems centering around contraception in respect to sexuality, to my mind, have nothing whatever to do with the relations of man and wife. They have to do rather with premarital and extra-marital relationships—and these involve problems of a most serious character, both for the individuals involved and for society itself. Before the development of reasonably reliable contraceptive techniques, there was always the fear of pregnancy in an extra-marital or premarital relation. Although fear has no justification as an ethical motive, it would be naive to deny its power in human behavior generally. There can be no doubt that in the past a great many people who were impelled to illicit sexual relations refrained from them for no other reason than fear. Reliable contraception has drastically changed this situation and introduced problems which are as a general proposition unique to our culture. For whereas, in the past, extra-marital sexual relations were frequently just that and had no implications with respect to emotional involvement, such relations today frequently tie together people who move in the same social circles and are often friends as families. Accordingly, they frequently "justify" themselves by convincing themselves that they have fallen in love with the other party to the extra-marital relation.

Surely in our culture, at least, such extra-marital relationships eat at the very roots of marriage ethically conceived. Yet at the same time, it is all too easy to take a holier than thou attitude toward people whose lives become thus complicated, and this self-righteousness may be no lesser a violation than the other. Understanding and compassion, too, have their place in the life of ethical judgment. When involvements of this kind do occur, however, the least one ought to expect is a readiness to take responsibility for all possible implications of the entanglement.

The problems of sexual behavior before marriage, while different, are in one sense no less difficult of solution with sound judgment. We did not need the Kinsey reports to let us know how widespread, and in some social groups indeed commonplace, is premarital sexual intercourse. On the one hand, it is no contribution to the ethical life to induce serious emotional and psychological difficulties in unmarried individuals in the name of Victorian chastity. On the other hand, sexual promiscuity ought to be an obvious violation of ethical standards. Again, at a minimum, any sexual relationship which is exploitive is clearly unethical. That is why prostitution—to say nothing of "sex crimes"—is basically offensive. No person ought ever to be merely *used* for the sexual satisfaction of another. So premarital sexual relationships, when they do occur, ought to be characterized by a deep sense of mutual respect for personality.

Let us turn now to the question of divorce. With respect to this question, as those just discussed, it is well for me to emphasize that there are differing views within the Ethical Culture Movement. For example, Felix Adler was rigidly opposed to divorce, as I am not. His opposition was so profound that he refused to officiate at the re-marriage of divorced persons. In effect, he would say: "People wish to dissolve a marriage, to divorce, because they reach the conclusion that they are incompatible. Who is compatible?

The problem of marriage is for two different or incompatible personalities to build an ethical relationship. Therefore, no marriage should ever be dissolved."

Great as is the respect I hold for Adler, I think his attitude on this matter is so irrelevant to much of human behavior as to be almost unethical in its absolutism. Insofar as marriage is *the* maturing relationship, whose aim is mutual development of the best in the two personalities involved, then when people become completely destructive of each other's personality to preserve the marriage is not to advance an ethical relationship, but to destroy it. Yet no person has the right to destroy another. When it becomes transparently clear, accordingly, that a marriage is irreparably destructive, then I think divorce is not only ethically justified but demanded.

For Ethical Culture, to move from considerations of personal and family life to those of religion is a logical one. I think that religion (or, as I prefer to say, a religious attitude toward life) is the most private dimension of human experience. In this deeply intimate sense, I do not believe that most people have the same kind of religion, and it may well be that, whatever general tenets one accepts, every person differs in his religious views just because of personality differences and differences in experience and inter- pretation. Aside from the associational and institutional character of religion, to which I shall turn in a moment, I believe that a religious view of life is something to be properly nourished in the family.

It has been my experience, particularly in this recent period of religious revival and conformist pressures, that a great many parents join a church in order to send their children to the Sunday School, because they think it is somehow good for the children to learn religion. Meantime, many of them do not attend church services, and some of them do not believe in the church's position at all. What frequently communicates to the child under these circum- stances is not what happens in the Sunday School, but the in- difference and even cynical attitude of the parents. I predict that many of these children will grow up to be, not religious adults, but nonreligious or even antireligious individuals. Religious education is effective for a child when it is an expression of the family's integrity. When this is the case, the child may change his point of view later in life, taking a position quite different from that of the parents; but he will respect the religion of his parents, as he will the parents themselves.

To be sure, many young adults who themselves had no religious identification as children are now becoming aware of a genuine religious need. For them, it is important that their children acquire a sense of religious identity. But there is no difficulty here, for it is an expression of that very family integrity which I have in mind.

If the family is where religious attitudes ought to be nurtured, then the church or religious institution ought really to be the instrumentality for the group celebration of shared attitudes and shared values, whatever they may be. Each of us needs to be identified with others, and especially to share with others those things which are most profound in our own lives insofar as they are sharable. That is why, granted the privacy of inner religious life, the religious institution is itself of major importance.

But if one grants that religion is essentially private in character and is to be nurtured in the family, then within the broadest possible limits the state should refrain from interfering in the religious life of its citizens. A given religious view can be completely misleading or completely wrong from your point of view or mine. It can be "a whoring after false gods." The state, nevertheless, has no right to interfere, unless the view in question holds a serious threat to the whole social structure. In saying this I am not referring merely to a democratic state. To my mind, the principle here stated is valid regardless of the nature of the state and regardless of the nature of the religion.

But there is the qualification just noted of threat to the social structure as such. It may be a snake cult in Florida, where a man in the course of what he regards as a religious observance is bitten by a poisonous snake and dies. Periodically we read in the newspapers of a child who is dying and whose life depends upon an operation, but whose parents will not sanction it because they regard any interference with natural developments as a defiance of God's will; in which case the physician or someone else may on occasion appeal to the courts to get legal sanction for proceeding with the necessary operation. Again, there was the practice of polygamy among the Mormons, which was so patently contrary to public policy and to prevailing attitudes in this country that the state had to intervene and abolish it. It is obviously a most difficult matter to determine at what point the state must intervene in order to preserve the social structure for which it exists. The courts of our country have been most chary in dealing with matters of this kind and most reluctant to make broad generalizations. Excepting such extremes as those just cited, I repeat that the state must permit the broadest possible freedom of expression, not only of religious but of nonreligious views, as well.

Now just as the state has an obligation to respect the ethical implications and practices of differing religious positions, so it also has the obligation to protect the rest of the community from having any one religious body dictate its morality. The protection of the Roman Catholic attitude toward divorce and contraception for the communicants of that church, for example, is a duty of the state. By the same token, the state has a duty to protect the rest of us from having the Roman Catholic view of morality on these questions become prescriptive for us.

Similar considerations are relevant to the problem of released time in the public schools for religious education; or, to go a step further, to the question of religious education itself in the public schools; or, to go still further, to the question of public financial assistance for parochial schools. In saying this, we must bear in mind that "released" time is quite different from what has been termed "dismissed" time. In the latter case, all children would be dismissed from school classes one or more hours a week in order that those whose families wished them to do so could go to the proper institution for religious education. If such additional time were all that the religious institutions advocating released time wanted, then they would logically be advocates of dismissed time. But this is not all they want. They are apprehensive that if all children were dismissed from school, then not nearly as many of them would come for special religious instruction as would be the case under a system of released time. It is obvious, therefore, that whatever the advocates of released time may say in defense of their position, they are actually using the institution of the public schools as one means of getting children to attend religious classes.

This whole matter may be summarized briefly, but I think not unfairly, as follows. When the churches found that an insufficient number of children were attending the regular Sunday morning services, then the institution of the Sunday School began to take hold. But the churches found, even with the Sunday Schools, that too many children were not involved in their programs. That is why the idea of released time arose as another expedient for gaining additional adherents among the children. In substance, it is as if the adults involved had said to themselves: "If the children will not come to us on Sunday mornings, then let us go where the children are during the week. Let us go to the school itself. Let us get them released from school early and take them by the hand or by special buses and bring them to the religious institution for the instruction they need." This seems to me to be a patent invasion of the system of public education in this country and it has no ethical justification whatever.

But the matter goes further than this. For released time, even when practiced on as wide a scale as at present, is thought insufficient. That is why there is so much current discussion about getting religion into the curriculum of the public schools themselves. The fact that the religious education of children ought to be a matter of major concern by no means warrants resort to the public schools as the answer to the problem. For aside from any other consideration, the alleged benefits of religious education in public schools would be vastly overbalanced by the difficulties involved in trying to keep lines clear in a culture as pluralistic religiously as is ours.

I find it most difficult to understand the proponents of a "core" religious curriculum. This would take whatever views are held in common by adherents of any facet of the Judeo-Christian tradition and present them to all children. On the face of it, this would be a violation of the freedom of belief of those families not adherents of the tradition. But from the viewpoint of those who are traditionally devout, I should think that the proposal would be basically offensive. If denominational differences are not thought to be of central importance, then why do the various denominations exist? If they are important, as they manifestly must be, then how can religion thus conceived be advanced by submerging that which is distinctive?

Accordingly, I think that from no point of view should the public schools be used for religious education of children. But the concern which underlies this proposal need not be ignored. The underlying problem can be dealt with in another way. In our culture there are shared ethical values—or, insofar as there are not, we should be moving in that direction. These values are properly part of a public school curriculum, since they ought to be integral to every child's education. What we need in the public schools of this country is not religious but ethical education.

Nor does the community, as organized in the state, have any right to use public funds for the forwarding of parochial or private education, in whatever way or under whatever guise it may be done. The corporate responsibility of society is to afford adequate facilities for the education of all children. If for religious or other reasons parents decide that they do not wish to have their children attend public schools, that is a matter of private judgment which must be respected by the community at large. But if I send my child to the Ethical Culture Schools, that does not absolve me from my more general community obligations to the public schools. Neither would it justify my asking the state to help finance the Ethical Culture Schools. The pity, of course, is that we have not achieved the kind of public education which would satisfy all different views and different values: which would cultivate genuine appreciation of the differences among people, which would not undermine but rather fortify people in their differing beliefs, and which would function on so high a level educationally that no just criticism could ever be made of the quality of the education there given. This is not presently the case, nor is it likely to be the case in the immediate future. Nevertheless, when parents send their children to private schools—whether for reasons of an educational, social, or religious nature—they have the responsibility themselves to support such enterprises.

In the prospectus of specific problems for discussion in this series of lectures, the question is raised of government initiative and private enterprise. When stated thus abstractly, there is insufficient ground for ethical judgment and there is accordingly no truly ethical question involved. For if the ethical concern is for the enrichment of personality and the prevention of its exploitation, economically as well as in other ways, then the ethical bearing of different systems of economic organization can be seen only specifically.

In the nineteenth century, for example, the rise of industrialism led to so cruel an exploitation of labor that any person of ethical sensitivity had to be concerned with the organization of labor and with possible government curtailment of the prerogatives of private enterprise. Partly out of just such concern, the Social Gospel movement developed in Protestantism. This was true also of the National Catholic Welfare Conference, and analogous developments were to be found among the Jewish groups. The Ethical Culture Movement, which was founded in this period, is to be seen in the perspective of this increasing concern with the ethical dimensions of human experience.

Since that time, our country has come a long way indeed. All the arguments in favor of the organization of labor are of course still relevant and valid. But by and large, and surely as seen against the relative developments among other peoples in the world, the workers of this country are no longer exploited. Such exceptions as the shameful treatment of migratory workers at the present time only point up this fact. This situation has created ethical problems of its own, quite different in kind from those of the earlier generation. For the strength of unionism in this country being what it is today, corruption among some labor officials and exploitation of their own membership by such officials, become matters of serious concern. Wholly aside from corruption, new problems have arisen, some of them of a most ironic character. So we have the strange spectacle of organizers for the A.F.L.-C.I.O., attempting to organize a union of their own in order to bargain collectively with the officers of the labor movement, and finding themselves bitterly opposed in their efforts by the chief proponents of labor organization!

Such considerations illustrate why it is impossible to generalize in these matters, and why ethical judgments can be made only in the context of specific economic problems. Whereas once the role of government with respect to labor organization was primarily if not exclusively to protect the right so to organize, there is now an emerging obligation for government to protect union members from their own officials. The organized labor movement, for example, is now accumulating pension funds in its treasuries which will soon be staggeringly large. Are the workers, individually and collectively, to whom these funds belong to have no proper guardianship of their interest in them? Years ago, the scandals among some of the large insurance companies in this country were so great that the state was forced to intervene and set up governmental machinery for the continuing supervision of such affairs. There can be no doubt that an analogous situation has now arisen in connection with pension funds in the labor movement.

To take another specific illustration: regardless of the economic or other reasons for it, it is obvious that private enterprise, as a matter of record, has not taken an ethical responsibility with respect to employment and unemployment. In bad times economically, a given corporation could, quite understandably, say that it had no right to squander its investors' funds for the sake of keeping un-needed employees on the payroll. Finally, the conscience of the community revolted against this state of affairs and demanded that government accept an obvious responsibility. That is why we now have unemployment insurance as a general practice in this country.

With pension funds, and improvement in the welfare of senior citizens generally, the situation is different. It is a mixed situation, pointing to a mixed approach economically. There is a degree to which private enterprise can and does take some of this responsibility. It cannot take it all. That is why the private responsibility must and is supplemented by governmental responsibility. In this case as in others it is not a matter of "either-or."

The fact is that Americans generally subscribe to a great myth. And this will do us no great harm as long as we understand some of the realities underlying it. The myth is that ours is a free-enterprise economy, and "free enterprise" is one of our shibboleths. This is so much the case that I have frequently felt the obligation to caution students from other parts of the world to tread carefully, while in this country, in any discussion of economic matters. For while the fact is that we are a mixed economy—of private, co-operative, and governmental enterprise—there is nothing many Americans will get more emotional about than anything that seems to indicate a "socialistic" questioning of free enterprise. Now while the theory of free enterprise was partly ethical in origin, being an economic expression of Adam Smith's moral philosophy, it was always irrelevant to the facts of life, because it never existed and never could exist as a matter of fact.

What is central to this question of the relation of government and private enterprise, to my mind, is not how much government or how much private enterprise may be involved in the total economy. It is rather a question of the morality of politics on the one side and the morality of business on the other. More especially, since we are a business society, the degree of corrupting relations and the extent of corrupting attitudes in the business system in which we live insidiously color the attitudes of the population as a whole. Impossible as it is to deal with this consideration in the present context, we should be mindful of the fact that this is an area of major ethical concern.

The question is also raised of the moral limits of the will to national survival. No nation is something external to its citizenry.

The individual and his society are obviously distinguishable. What is sometimes perhaps not so obvious is that the society of which the individual is part is in turn part of what the individual is. We not only live in a given culture; we *are* partly that culture. We all speak a common language, however differently each of us may speak it. Yet we do not merely "speak" our language. How we think—and in a measure how we act—is influenced by the nature of the language itself. For this and collateral reasons we can talk meaningfully of differences in national character. For all the endless variations within a given culture, there is a difference between the American character and the English character, between the English and the German, and so on. These national characters, of course, are to be understood as being descriptive and not prescriptive. They do not prescribe what ought to be the case, but they do describe what actually happens.

For a culture is a central part of any individual's integrity. Patriotism, accordingly, is not to be confused with jingoism; it is rather a sober realization of what oneself is. It is not to identify with Stephen Decatur's old dictum: "Our country! . . . may she always be in the right; but our country, right or wrong." It is rather to subscribe to Carl Schurz's amended statement: "My country, right or wrong; when right to keep her right; when wrong to set her right."

What, then, are the moral limits to the will to national survival? One generalization is clear, if not tautologous. If one knew that his nation could survive only at the cost of the destruction of mankind then not only would it be self-defeating and thus a form of madness; it would be ethically wrong. Felix Adler used to say that one's rights exist in an organism of rights. To seek one's own survival at the expense of all others is to destroy the very possibility of an ethical life. When an individual's life is threatened, he may justify killing his attacker on grounds of self-preservation. Yet that act of self-preservation is justified ethically, in turn, only as it is consistent with the larger framework of ethical values. This proposition is equally valid when applied to nations.

It is easy to generalize about the ethical conditions of national survival, but the generalization points to sobering considerations. Every act of war is a brutalization of human beings. All warfare is destructive of the ethical life of the human community. For years—and especially nowadays—we have talked at great length about how another war would lead to the destruction of civilization. I think we have not fully realized how much of civilization has actually been destroyed during the past forty years: the degree to which people can no longer genuinely communicate with each other; the extent to which their consciences have become desensitized; the manner in which hostilities have undermined the appreciation of one another by peoples who are different and whose differences ought to be mutually creative.

The extreme implication of the question of national survival, taken literally, will hardly be presented to us. I say this because I do not think that the ultimate weapons of warfare, which have been developed in our time, will ever be used. I think the strategy of terror through which we have been living cancels itself out. Just as poison gas was not used in World War II because of the twofold fear of contamination of one's own people and of retaliation in kind, so I do not think that we shall use the intercontinental ballistic missiles and hydrogen bombs which we have developed. For whatever else may be dictated by military strategy, the planning staff of any nation never invites disaster. It may be mistaken in its judgments, and its plans may unwittingly lead to disastrous results. But it will not plan for disaster. That is why I think the ultimate weapons will not be used.

Granted this, the difficult ethical problem rests with the consideration that any kind of war involves man's brutalization. I suspect this is a problem we are not going to solve in our lifetime. And that brings us back to the role of frustration in the ethical life; frustration seen now not simply as part of one's individual experience but in the broader context of intergroup and international life. Despite the frustrations of the past and the present with respect to creating a durable peace, the frustrations themselves must be seen as a possible occasion for ethical development. A peace which is not merely the absence of war but an active appreciation of the differences among the peoples of the world may never come. Yet the effort itself to achieve it, in and through the very frustrations that all people will experience, is an indispensable part of the ethical growth of mankind.

V

RATIONAL ETHICS

BY

LYMAN BRYSON

*Professor Emeritus of Education, Teachers College,
Columbia University*

This lecture is an attempt to state the principles supporting any
system of ethics which is essentially rational. What is their source
and what arguments can be offered to prove that they are valid?
To begin, we have to clear the ground.

A purely rational ethics cannot depend for its impulse on the
sanctions of immortality and it cannot claim divine revelation
as its guidance. This raises the first question to which we have
to offer an answer. What is the relation between rationalism and
religious belief? To pass this by, as if it did not matter, would be
to leave all kinds of possible misunderstandings. The man who
undertakes to rule his life by reason is not bound, I think, to explain his religious beliefs in order to justify his behavior. I would
condemn as an example of wicked spiritual pride the attitude of
those who say that they cannot believe in a man's virtue in action
unless they can approve his sanctions. This is almost as evil as
the attitude of those who deny to some of their human brothers
the possibility of being good men because they hold what these
self-appointed judges call evil ideas. The man in action need not
explain; his actions speak for him. But the theorist has to explain;
that is his business.

The rationalist as we find him in the world may or may not be
a follower of a creed, a member of a religious communion. There

are rational principles in all religious systems, as the papers presented to this Institute have indicated. But we are talking about the possibility of acting on a purely rational basis in spite of, or without the help of, religious teachings. The theoretical rationalist—for whom in all these things I shall speak dogmatically, to save time, although I have full realization of the number of reasoning men who would reject me as their spokesman—believes that the religious impulse, in all its forms, no matter how primitive in expression or how mature and profound, is always a faith that there is an ultimate harmony between the nature of the universe and man's dim ideas of justice, mercy, and righteousness. He may suffer the agonies of Job and be awed into accepting the powers of God, or he may give thanks for happiness, but he holds to this faith no matter what happens in his own span of time. This is the ultimate basis of religious emotion, deep in all creeds. The rationalist may feel this emotion or be without it. One distinguished modern philosopher said, "There is no cosmic plan which aims at man's survival or at achieving his ideals for to his lot the universe is morally indifferent." [1] From him to the observant Christian or Jew, all rationalists will agree on the basis of their ethics. The basis is in reason. This makes it impossible, of course, for their ethics to be fixed or explicit in a system or a set of rules. That there are profound differences of opinion among representative spokesmen for this point of view is not accidental; differences in personal thinking are in the character of the rational approach to the problems of life.

Some deeply religious persons have envied the rationalist his freedom from system, suspecting perhaps that God might work more directly through man's own reason than by external manifestations and promises. The great rationalizers of religious faiths, such as St. Thomas Aquinas and Maimonides, have seemed at times to feel that they could make a better case for righteousness and a better case for God's ultimate justice by showing how He worked through human reason as the most divine thing in His creature, rather than through voices or the signs of wrath. And

[1] Nagel, Ernest, *Logic Without Metaphysics,* Free Press, Glencoe, Ill., 1957, p. 50.

there is that wonderful story told by Joinville about the Crusaders who met in the streets of Constantinople an old woman carrying a pail of water and a flaming torch. These, she said, were to put out the fires of Hell and burn down Heaven so that men would be righteous for the sake of righteousness and not for either fear or hope of reward.

The rationalist may get no help from creeds: his freedom is his danger and his burden. He must seek wisdom not only where it is written but where it is essential in the truths of experience. This is a much more difficult quest than to look out for the true word or the teacher. It requires examination of all the words, indeed, and all the teachings, unless a rationalist is bold enough to think he can generate the answers out of his own brief experience. He may insist on his freedom to differ but he has freedom also to agree and he has to decide on his own system. The interpretation of experience is in his opinion man's highest privilege, but it is also his heaviest responsibility.

The religious impulse is not the same thing as religion. If we speak of a system of judgments based on religion we do not mean anything so formless as the relation between a man's conviction that the universe is ultimately righteous and the rules by which he behaves. We mean a system of behavior which has its evident roots in those social habits and tools the religious impulse leads men to create. We mean churches or institutional religious collectivities. A religious sanction for a judgment on action may be based on revelation, on supernatural sanction, on the rules of a sacred community—on any or all of these. There is much confusion in usage here, as is natural since men do not want to push their thinking about the sanctions of action too far in finite distinctions. Since we are discussing the good and evil of human action from the point of view of the professing rationalist we have to be somewhat more strict. We will, then, make the arbitrary distinctions that are necessary. We will speak of three levels or kinds of "ought" judgments. They are all natural; they are all common to the experience of normal human beings and I do not intend to hint at any hierarchy of validity or importance. But they are distinguishable, even though any living man might find it difficult to locate the three aspects of judgment in any decision which he would call "moral."

The religious "ought" judgment, then, is based on supernatural sanctions which are expressed in human organizations that have their origin in what I have called the religious impulse.

The moral judgment, strictly speaking, is an expression of the customs of a tribe. We have to disregard here, in order to be clear, the common and wholly permissible use of the word "moral" to cover all kinds of "ought" judgments no matter what the sanctions or the importance of the question. The general use of the word moral to cover all such judgments is the more natural because in our normal experience the influence of the customs of the tribe tends to extend over or to absorb other considerations. The relation between a religious judgment, for example, and a moral judgment, in this strict sense, is very close. Often they are so interwoven in the conscience and the imagination that no casuist could disentangle them. In the conduct of our lives, of course, there is no reason for separating them. This closeness led one anthropologist, Durkheim, to identify the religious impulse with the spirit of the collectivity, the spirit of the tribe.

There are in every social group, however, sets of precepts, rules, customs of more or less compulsory force, which are not sacred. In primitive societies they may be more difficult to extricate from the nexus of the tribe and the religious community, as indeed they were difficult sometimes to separate from each other in the ancient city-states where families were surrogate chapels of the state cult. In civilized societies, and in the subcultures of sophisticated groups, the trivial ends of this continuum shade off into manners. Where there has been great solidarity of belief and practice, the continuum has run from religious sanctions at one end to manners at the other with no clear disjunction anywhere. This is, of course, quite uncommon in modern Western societies; the resident of New York or Paris is not likely to have any doubt as to the difference between a religious duty and a duty owed to his social standing or his honor.

The third kind of ought judgment, what I will call an ethical judgment, has, strictly speaking, no sanctions outside the self. A transgression will not be punished by an offended Deity, nor by an outraged tribe. The transgressor is more likely to be puzzled than shamed. And it is in this phase of judgment that reason is the only source of light or assistance.

There is also reason in religion, and morals are reasonable. If we follow the advice of Aristotle, and of all the religious teachers known to me, we will say that religious teachings and moral teachings should begin in childhood and should be made elements in the "habits"—this is Aristotle's word—of the child. The philosopher implied that there were other questions, of the kind we have called "ethical" which would be the subject-matter of the contemplation which is man's highest sphere of action.

Even the most aggressive rationalist would not contend, I think, that all the rules of conduct, along the whole continuum from sacred usages to manners, should be thought and argued through afresh by each human being for himself. This would be an intolerable waste of time and power. Whatever can properly be called a mere "custom" is to be followed, as Pascal said, merely because it is a custom. The reasoning powers should be saved for important problems and the more the trivial and commonplace phases of life can be made into routines the better.

This, however, only gets us into deeper difficulties if we do not go on, since the kind of question which is settled by appeal to religious sanctions is not usually trivial and may be of the most profound significance in life. What the stubborn rationalist would ask, I think, is this: Are these questions really or ultimately questions of conduct? Do they involve in any significant degree an "ought" judgment? Are they not rather questions regarding the meaning of spiritual experiences, judgments on the universe and human destiny, rather than judgments on mortal behavior?

When we consider the nature of these distinctions and realize fully the extent to which the three aspects of good and evil action are intertangled in ordinary self-examinations, or in our more instinctual choices, we are bound, by rational principles, to look also at the question of motivation. In the person who lives under the influence of all three—religion, morals, and ethics—the motives for his choices will undoubtedly be of diminishing strength in that succession. What he thinks of as sanctioned by religion will be strongest, what is arrived at by analysis and intellectual judgment will be faintest and least colored by emotion. The rationalist who is also a naturalist and without religious commitment may say that this gives the ethical judgment the best chance of being useful and constructive for humanity. If supernatural ends are disregarded, the judgment arrived at without emotional involvement is more likely to be clear. For reasons which I hope to make evident, there is a good deal of truth in this; there is great value to the progressing world in the increase of knowledge and the enlargement of the areas of rational as distinguished from passional judgments. But there is reason for pause here also.

The question is somewhat more complex than it seems. We do not know how much the pure rationalist is carried forward toward action by the religious motivation which he inherited from earlier and more observant or more overtly and institutionally religious ancestors. Indeed, we do not know how much the loyalty to the "ought" judgment itself may be an inheritance from ancient and ostensibly abandoned religious teaching. We do not know this because we have no history of a time when religious beliefs had died out in naturalism and civilization had gone on long enough to test the strength of ethical motives left without even an inherited trace of that emotional support.

In spite of the fact that our contemporaries belong to churches and congregations, and attend services more often than did our ancestors, it would not be maintained, I am sure, that religious practices have the hold upon the lives and motives of the intellectual leaders of our culture that they once had. It is my own strong conviction for which I can adduce plenty of historical evidence that these intellectual and artistic leaders live by principles as pure and generous and useful to mankind as those which animated their ancestors who had more immediate religious guidance. But it is evident that many of these men and women learned their morals—if not their ethics—from parents and teachers who did obey religious sanctions. They inherited the motivations without the sanctions. I do not believe that any positivistic rationalist can be quite sure that when this inheritance runs out the "ought" judgments will be made and acted on by the motivations of reason alone. No one knows.

The rationalist depends for his confidence in reason alone on two basic principles. First, man is a gregarious animal who gets his natural happiness out of association with his kind. Second, the increase of knowledge, any kind of knowledge, works ultimately for human betterment.

To discuss these principles, we must have some kind of definition or common idea of the good, the secular good, that is, the good which can be achieved in our lifetime on earth beyond which this kind of reasoning cannot take us. Whether religious or not, in any of the senses which I have indicated, the rationalist will believe that there is no necessary conflict between his good and the good of the man who lives by a creed, whose guidance is by revelation and whose motivation is the sanction of an after-life reckoning. He can accept a definition of the good which would fit the aims of any religious teacher who believes, as he must, that life on earth can be made healthy and pure and rewarding in itself, whatever bearing it may have on Heaven or Hell.

I would suggest that the rationalist can find a definition to work with in the words of Thomas Hill Green. It is not necessary to follow him in all his Hegelian spiritualism to agree with his formulation. Green says:

In the broad result it is not hard to understand how man has bettered himself through institutions and habits which tend to make the welfare of all the welfare of each, and through the arts which make nature, both as used and as contemplated, the friend of man. And just so far as this is plain, we know enough of ultimate moral good to guide our conduct; enough to judge whether the prevailing interests which make our character are or are not in the direction which tends further to realize the capabilities of the human spirit.[2]

The critical clause for which I value Green's definition is this: "man has bettered himself through institutions and habits which tend to make the welfare of all the welfare of each, and through the arts which make nature, both as used and as contemplated, the friend of man." As to the effectiveness of reason in achieving the good defined in the second part of this sentence there can be no question, and I think we need not spend time in demonstration. Indeed, it is often a complaint against the rationalist and the scientist and the positivist that they have made nature too much the friend of man. They have subdued material forces to the service of man until, we are told, man has lost the moral values of austerity and is too comfortable. They have, at the same time, indulged too much man's childish love of destruction and given him weapons that outrage morality. They have saved him to live a long life not holy enough to deserve lengthening. The rationalist has no sympathy with all these complaints; he finds them almost wholly baseless and unjust. But he finds in them also the grudging admission that reason does achieve mastery of nature and he remembers that many of the advances in scientific knowledge have had to be made in the face of intolerance by religious authorities.

The difficult question for the rationalist in ethics to answer is suggested by the first part of the sentence from Green. Has reason in human affairs helped to establish those "institutions and habits which tend to make the welfare of all the welfare of each"? In other words, does reason lead us to love our neighbors as ourselves?

For an adequate examination of such a question we should have to cover all of history to find all the periods—brief, most of them— in which reason had a chance and this would try your patience and show up my ignorance. But we can look for a moment at the beginning of modern times.

[2] Green, Thomas Hill, *Prolegomena to Ethics* (ed. by A. C. Bradley) 4th ed., Oxford, Clarendon Press, 1899, p. 204.

In the seventeenth century, the "century of genius," modern rationalism was founded on the ruins of scholasticism, and modern science, which is the natural fruit of rationalism, was also founded when the notions of mechanism and measure were introduced into the study of nature. In the seventeenth century, the crust of seeming solidarity which had been formed by the rituals of church and state over the seething conflicts of the Middle Ages had been broken open by Reformation, Counter Reformation, and Renaissance. The intellectual debris was swept away and the new world mapped out by Spinoza, Descartes, and Leibnitz. The modern world, not only modern science but philosophy also, and the common sense thinking of the modern kind, such as we find in America more than elsewhere, is all constructed of ideas of process, of the flow of energy through temporal forms; the scholastic base of substance and attribute was henceforth meaningless.

It took the rationalists a generation to make this change. Spinoza, with innocent ruthless logic, showed that if substance exists there must be one fully realized substance of which all the phenomena of human experience are merely partial realizations and that one substance is both God and Nature, *Deus sive Natura*. Substance then becomes a meaningless word. And Leibnitz showed, also with inescapable cogency, that substance—if it exists at all—must be infinitely divisible. Hence reality is an infinite number of monads or separate substances among which there can be no communion or interaction. And substance becomes an absurdity in that direction also. Two great minds, working in opposite directions, one to show that if there is substance there can be only one, the other to show that if there is substance there must be an infinite number of independent substances, made the notion of substance impossible.

From then on, for a long time, philosophy in the West was the biography of this notion's ghost. Men were afraid that giving up the idea of substance would be to give up the basis for a belief in the reality of their own souls and they shrank from that sacrifice. Spinoza did not shrink. He saw that his own thinking must necessarily modify the idea of the soul and he gave up personal immortality because the claim seemed to him an impertinence to

God. Leibnitz was more flexible. He used all the subtleties of his great mind to prove things which a modern rationalist, and many religious thinkers also, would say did not need to be proved. But the reaction against substance was swung so far that in our time an eminent metaphysician has hypostasized *attributes*. In fact, Whitehead calls God the principle of Concretion, at which Spinoza might smile and murmur—*sive Natura,* recognizing a subtle form of his own pantheism.

With all this, the rationalist has sympathy, whatever he may follow as metaphysical faith. He knows that men want the solidity of an absolute, somewhere in the universe, and if there is no such thing as "substance" there must be something equivalent. If there is no absolute, when discourse has got through with analyzing experience, then it is necessary to invent one. The physicists, having analyzed absolute space and time out of being, comfort themselves with the absolute velocity of light. The rationalist tries not to forget that metaphysics, like the other arts, is not only a way of getting at the truth but also a conductor for the lightnings of emotion.

To go back again to the seventeenth century, it was Descartes who took the philosophical step which made modern science possible. I believe that we may some day come to see that he made a modern rational ethics possible also, by the same stroke. I do not mean in his mathematical and other strictly scientific speculations; in these he was surpassed by Leibnitz. I mean in his famous dichotomy, or dualism, which some have blamed him for on moral grounds or for logical reasons.

What he did was to extricate the body from the soul. This was a tremendous forward step in human thought, because it reversed the secular trend of the thinkers who, since Plato at least, had been trying to extricate the soul from the body. This was attempted in order to give the soul freedom for righteousness. It is most familiar to us in the fevered words of St. Paul. But all through early Christian times and the Middle Ages, it was taken for granted that there was an immortal soul housed in some uneasy fashion in a physical body and corrupted by its flesh.

It was not for moral reasons that Descartes made the separation. He separated from this marriage of body and soul the tangible part because that would make it possible for us to understand that tangible part, at least, even if we could not fully comprehend the soul. It has been supposed that he did this in simple logical error. This seems to me unlikely. He had good reason to extricate the body from any consideration of the spiritual aspect of man's experience since he wanted to think of the body as a machine. It was by explicitly denying that he thought man's mind, *i.e.,* his spirit or soul, was mechanical, that he could hope to go any further with his physiological speculations. The authorities of Church and State would have closed his mouth with brutal dispatch if he had not cleared away that possible misunderstanding. We cannot tell whether he did it only for self-protection, or only to isolate that part of the human personality which could perhaps be freely examined, or perhaps because, as scientist, he naturally began with a gross analysis, a division of his subject, the human being, into manageable parts. In any case he made it possible to study the human body as a mechanism, and all of modern biology and medicine hang on that. If the dualism of Descartes was a mistake, it was one of the fruitful mistakes in the history of thought.

If my violent simplification of the complex and subtle interrelations of seventeenth century thought can be accepted as a working scheme of ideas (not as historical or critical comment on the philosophers summarily treated), it may be possible to extend these ideas into our own time and thinking. I believe that modern ethical ideas are arrived at by an almost discernible road from medicine to the study of the interplay of soma and psyche, to mental health, to freedom of the spirit. I do not believe that this frees us from the eternal problem of good and evil but it can well show us how to diminish the number of those we call evil men and even to cure the evil in our own hearts.

I say we are not required to follow Green in his spiritualistic interpretation of human destiny and the living universe, but it may be useful to try to state what the rationalist who is also a positivist, who relies on reason alone and not on religious sanctions, thinks of the relation between what were called in the time of Descartes, the body and the soul. Before Descartes, as I say, these two entities, these two parts of human nature, had been thought of as eternally in combat. Rationalism and science have since then partly overcome this idea. But it is still among the less seriously enforced elements in some creeds and it dominated American culture for a long time in the form of Puritanism. The rationalist who follows the completely naturalistic position of Nagel as quoted, or of philosophers like Santayana, cannot be a Puritan.

To be a Puritan, the rationalist would have to think of the universe as a friend but treat his own body as an enemy. Both Plato, the great philosophical spring of Christian doctrine, and Paul who built the early church out of his own body's sufferings, made this distinction but that does not convince the rationalist. It is not a logical inconsistency that he rejects although he would, from a modern point of view, say that his own body was the part of nature which was closest to him, and the most typical sample of nature he could ever know. If his own heart and nerves were his enemy he could not look comfortably for a friend in the whirlwind or the galactic distances. He might feel some sympathy with Montaigne's refusal to think of himself as a fully orthodox believer on this account, although for other reasons he would have to refuse help in this matter from Aristotle whose ideas of balance comforted Montaigne. No, it would be other reasons, basically perhaps a feeling of natural loyalty that would make him insist that his body was his friend.

His feeling of trust in the harmony between his own soul and the universe has already been explained as his essential impulse toward religious emotions, toward awe and gratitude for life and an ache for righteousness. He knows that his body may sometimes betray him. So may any other part of this indescribable and unanalyzable self betray the whole of it. His weary nerves may betray his judgment, his eager appetites his virtue, and his esurient brain may confuse the facts of the world outside him. But so also may his false judgments thwart the wisdom of the body and waste the powers he needs for good deeds. A mistake in the ordinary business of living, in driving a car, or buying food, may destroy him. The life of the whole self hangs on the intelligence as well the loyalty of all the parts.

Has he then no higher and lower nature which contend with one another? Perhaps, but not in the Platonic sense, as two horses, one headed downward and one upward, requiring control by a driver. Who is the driver? He finds some of his most powerful impulses toward what his ultimate conscience calls goodness coming from deep in the nervous system wherein he has locked away memories and experience. Even in the Platonic sense he believes in the reality of his soul only when the soul is conceived as the whole being of which all the parts of him, physical events, essences, and engrammed recordings, make when they are put together. Putting them together would be one of the greatest feats of the imagination if we had to analyze it. But just as we make both wholes and universals of unorganized experiences, so we learn in our first years to create a "self" in the midst of life. This is the only soul he can rationally find.

The Burmese medicine man told his disciples and worshippers that he could see a butterfly leave the lips of a dying man; it was the man's soul. This is a crude poetic attempt to satisfy the mind to whom Plato's definition of "reality" was inadequate. The rational man I am describing does not need the butterfly. He also does not need to give any other kind of form or substance to the soul; the soul is the whole being, the Platonic idea of the self. One can follow Plato and call it "real" since real is a value word and can be allotted as we choose. But if the soul, as the whole self, the essential idea of the person, is real it cannot be real in the same sense as is the body or the historical events in the body's career.

It may also be immortal as a sunset is immortal or a beautiful act, or a heavenly sound. Ideas have no material physical existence; material existences are only their temporary exemplifications. The rational man thinks he sees in the logic of the universe that whatever has a beginning has also an end; his soul was always an idea hence it has neither beginning nor end. It is immortal but its sentient experience which is its sign disappears as does the colored atmosphere of the sunset or the event in time which a man calls a good deed.

This disposes for the rational man of the notion of the soul as a kind of police blotter or supernatural report card on which are written up his balanced credits and debits, to be processed through a divine Hollerith machine and thence to produce a profile of his eternal destiny. One often gets an idea much like this in reading the sermons and moral tales of the early Middle Ages and indeed even Dante can be read in this way if one misses the profound concept of the soul which Dante put into drama and Thomas Aquinas into syllogisms. This simple idea of the soul is often found among devout men and women even now. It may be that it comes out of a failure ever to attain to a sense of whole being, a fully realized sense of self. It is quite possible, as has been shown by fine minds in all the churches and religions, to feel an accountability to a personal God who is *in* the universe, not a God who is simply another name for the universe, without thinking of the soul as a ghost marked with sin for eternity or washed by virtue, but it must be admitted that few theologians or religious mystics can show evidence that they use these words with any rational meaning. If they are content with mystery, that is, of course, a proper use of their spiritual freedom; the rational man shows his essential temper at this point again. He knows that he cannot ultimately understand the working of life and fate and the external world; but he refuses to give names to his defeats and call them answers.

It is fair for others to ask of the rationalist whether or not he thinks these forerunners in the seventeenth century left him anything worth having for his ethical system. Did the Enlightenment, with its irenic iconoclasms, leading to modern science with its prodigious contribution to man's enjoyment of nature for both use and contemplation, help him toward righteousness? Did it help him to identify his own welfare with the welfare of all?

His answer would be, I think, that it did and that the spirit of science itself moves men toward mutual understanding and ultimate brotherhood. He might insist—I would—that the important word in Green's sentence may be "contemplation." To understand nature is more important to man than to bend nature's energies to human purposes. In this Aristotelian judgment, the rationalist would be affirming in another way his belief that human reason is the greatest of human qualities, and that learning is the greatest of human actions—not learning for the sake of use but for its own sake. And this is part of his ethical thinking because it indicates his ultimate scale of values. But it is not part of the case he undertakes to make out in behalf of his ethics. He would say rather, on the point at issue, that modern science is the direct product of the thinking of the seventeenth century and that anyone who ponders the writings of Spinoza or Leibnitz or Descartes, the three founders mentioned, or those of Galileo and Bacon, will find foreshadowed the spirit of modern ethics as well as the spirit of modern science. That spirit is a humble but confident tolerance. Being without fear, it can escape being cruel, and by being devoted to a public form of truth, it can accept others as they are. I am not saying this only of the social sciences which have grown up after the physical sciences; I am saying it of the physical sciences themselves and of the institutions and habits which have developed in the world as a result of the activities of those dedicated to their study.

It is often said, these days, that we have gone much further in developing our knowledge of the material world and in the mastery of material forces, in achieving the second part of Green's definition of moral progress, than we have in improving human behavior. I am not prepared to admit the truth of this complaint. To me it smells of both self-righteousness and sentimentality. It is sentimental because it sees the past in a haze of filial piety which misrepresents the behavior of our fathers. It is self-righteous because it assumes moral superiority on the part of the complainant. Rabbi Louis Finkelstein, with a candor hard to find in theologians, has said:

Like an orphaned child, who imagines that if he had a mother he would give her all his love and duty, so we, living in an age of shaken faith, suppose that given unquestioning belief, the world's moral problem would be solved. The man of antiquity knew better. Absolutely convinced as he was of God's existence, power, and omniscience, he yet found it impossible to escape from sin.[3]

We ought to be willing to face the fact that history, as distinguished from pious memory, does not find much virtue in our ancestors. I believe, on the grounds of my own years of reading and observation, that the general behavior of men in the Western world has steadily improved. It is not yet good enough. If it were, we should not be talking about ethics, or about morals. There is, however, a point of importance involved in this anxiety about our slow progress in behavior, even if one is bound by the facts to admit that it is progress.

The point is that we do not have, in our modern Western culture, especially in the United States as the most advanced example of the type, such a dedication of fine minds and studious lives to the study of values as we once had. It was not so long ago that a very large number of our best imaginations and most logical brains were engaged in the study and improvement of human values. These persons were the heads of educational institutions; college presidents now are administrators, if not actually businessmen, dedicated no doubt but busy with pragmatic affairs. Or the fine minds were in the ministry. The churches now are full, but are the ablest men attracted to the ministry? Religious leaders say no. Or these persons in earlier days might have been poets, novelists, dramatists, devoted to the exploration of moral values and ethical problems. The literary fashion of our time is a rash immorality which is not justified by ethical seriousness. Where are the logical minds and the imaginative minds which were once devoted to the study and advancement of human values?

The best minds now are mostly in science. The greater opportunities for education and for cultural experience have undoubtedly brought into full development a much larger proportion of potential talent, of all kinds, in our modern American culture than was ever encouraged before or elsewhere. Our equali-

[3] Finkelstein, Louis, *The Pharisees,* Jewish Publication Society of America, Philadelphia, 1940, Vol. I, p. 166.

tarian manners may offend the intellectuals of Europe, but those manners and the generosity of educational opportunity in America have brought enormous numbers of talents into fruition. They have also brought into self-expression great numbers of second and third and fifth rate talents and this obscures the achievement, especially to the observation of strangers. But first rate brains have also been discovered and have been helped to discover themselves.

It is not necessary to say here that great discoveries in science and great advances in technology are the products of brave imagination. But this imaginative courage is trained to seek generalizations which can be verified in external sensory experience and applied to material entities. As Cohen and Nagel put it, the scientist trusts his method and accepts whatever it brings him. I have myself defined science as description without adjectives of value. No matter how we define his activity, the scientist uses his powers to make generalizations which may or may not serve human values but he seeks to satisfy only one human value, the love of truth. And no matter how the motives of any scientific or technological worker may be enlightened by humane considerations, he submits his results to a completely objective test whenever he can and accepts its verdict. He has no private scientific truth and he is, in this home area, wholly positivistic. What is not proved may not be assumed to be true. Statements about entities which are not subject to proof by sensory testing are not merely unproved, they are meaningless.

We have to face the fact that we may have lost greatly in the beauty and worth of our lives by reason of this migration of gifted persons from the world of values into the world of positive truths. But what have we gained? It is my own belief that in one field at least, the field here under discussion, ethics, we have greatly gained. I believe that human conduct has, on the whole, been improved by the scientific trend of our day by two factors. Enthusiasm has been sobered. The kind of ignorance which leads to fear and thence to cruelty has been diminished. The rationalist who is trying to build an ethics without revelation and without transcendental sanctions would say that this is evidence to show that the human reason will lead to ethical good if it is allowed to follow its own bent toward learning everything possible about nature and man.

It may be, of course, that this is another example of a rule long believed in, namely, that the greatest goods are attained indirectly. Seek wisdom and find happiness. That can be rewritten: seek knowledge and find righteousness.

And if one wants to put this in religious terms I would say this: it takes a more profound trust in the ultimate righteousness of the universe, faith in God if one wants to use those words, to believe that man will get closer to his own deep convictions of justice and mercy by studying the material manifestations of the universe around him, than by conning over the attempts at ethical judgment and moral wisdom of his ancestors who often stumbled badly even when they were laying the foundations of the knowledge on which he now works. This may be, in the opinion of some theologians, an impious statement; I would insist that it is not an irreligious one.

There is, I believe, a direct gain, of the utmost importance, in the drawing off of imagination and power into the realm of science, where truth is the only value sought for. To describe it we have to go back to the basic factors in the first great ethical struggle of which we have any record outside religious tradition; the record in the writings of two of the supremely gifted minds in Western history, Plato and his pupil. It is difficult to translate precisely into modern English terms the substantives of value which Plato and Aristotle used. "Justice" is something more than giving to each what he deserves or has a right to; it means also order and harmony. "Temperance" is more than mere regulation of appetite; it is also modesty of passion. Plato tried to show how the Socratic dialectic, used in the instruction of men of all ages but solidly built into an educational system, would have led to justice and temperance and modesty in these terms, to musically harmonious grace of action, to fortitude and courage, to civic devotion, and private purity and friendship. Aristotle, in his more explicit way of thinking, made his inventory of the virtues and their complementary vices to show that excess of any virtue was vicious and that moderation, between the extremes, was always the path of magnanimous righteousness. This has often been misunderstood, even by historians, to indicate that the Greeks held moderation in ideal respect and practiced it in their essential Greekness. The contrary is, of course, the truth. They were so lacking in moderation that their gifts destroyed them.

These ancient wise men knew something about human character and destiny which has seldom been taken with enough seriousness; they offered rules which have almost never been obeyed. The sober, law abiding servant of God in the Judaic tradition, the meek and loving brother of all in the Christian tradition, were temperate, no doubt, but they have been overwhelmed in history over and over again by those who were passionately intemperate in good causes and there have never been lacking rabbis, priests, and ministers to infuriate men and to drive them on.

Modern scholarship has done something to remind us of what we had forgotten, that the Greeks had religions of superstition and irrational mysticism along with the pursuit of quiet restraint by the minority of the wise. It may even be said, with all the caution which any reconstruction of history demands, that Christianity might have had less bloody beginnings and been less stained by massacres, pogroms, and altars of human torches and—to come right down to our own country and not so long ago—of hanged Quakers, if it had had more in it of temperance and justice and less of enthusiasm. It is often said with irresponsible assurance that there would never have been a Christian church without martyrs. That may be true except for the fact that it implies that there had to be martyrs to heresy, to dissident beliefs, and to anticlerical rebellion, as well as martyrs of the faith.

The old Greek teachers knew that man's passions are not to be trusted even when they are enlisted in a holy cause, perhaps least of all when they are so engaged. What we have now is a chance to test the possibility and the value of a culture in which enthusiasm will be lessened because able men are devoted to the pursuit of objective truth rather than to the achievement of enthusiastic dreams of ideal good.

It is a bold stand to take, to say that this is an age in which enthusiasms may diminish and that thereby the chance of destructive enthusiasms—Aristotle would have asked, Are there any other kinds?—are also diminished. It is a bold thing to say to men who remember Buchenwald and Hiroshima and other crimes committed for bad causes and for good causes, an age of wars and hatreds and suspended fear. I believe nevertheless that it is so.

We can take as our next step a working definition of ethical success. We cannot rely on mere moral success if we stick to the arbitrary distinction between morals and ethics. A moral life in our sense is a way of wisely seeking happiness. The favorable judgment of one's peers and companions is part of rational happiness and I think it is quite certain that prudence is a moral virtue even though it may not be an ethical one. On the other hand, if ethical conduct may be "immoral," if an ethical judgment, an act of the higher righteousness by any system of ethics, is something which transcends the immediate judgment of one's companions, even though it may appeal to their higher selves, it is indifferent to prudential happiness. The martyr and the saint are neither moral nor happy in the ordinary meanings of those words because they have made a vocation of acting on ethical principles rather than moral rules.

Ethical success, then, cannot be the same as living what one's neighbors call a "good life." On the other hand, it does not mean necessarily to reject the morals of one's tribe and go whoring after strange gods. It means, I think, on the highest level, a friendly sympathy with morals and even a friendly acquaintance with those elements in the surrounding moral atmosphere that are seen to be mere conformity. In the terms of modern social psychology, following Riesman, this means that the "other directed" person is not capable of ethical success, no matter what his behavior, because he is not capable of an ethical judgment which is anything more than a moral judgment. He follows the crowd and is good in that degree. The crowd may be a righteousness fellowship and his behavior may be pure and kind; he is still not an ethical success because he has made no real ethical choice. He has merely accepted what, by his good luck, was righteousness.

This is not to deny the deep wisdom of the tribe. The morals of living groups of men and women are in most cases the residue of long experience and there is a rough survival of the fittest among moral systems. In little pockets of primitive life one can find societies whose morals are self-destructive, repressive, and by any ethical judgment evil. They are poisoned by sorcery and cruelty and inflict unnecessary pain. There are also elaborate and noble religions, such as Hinduism, which comprise customs of profound and rationally unnecessary cruelty because the logical interpretation of their religious systems, based, they believe, on revelation and personal knowledge of God, has led them to cruelty. The Hindu widow, until *sutee* was stopped by the British raj, was burned alive on her husband's funeral pyre. But aside from appalling exceptions of these kinds, which should not too much distort the picture of natural customs, the tribal morals of all societies are full of worldly wisdom. The rationalist believes this, perhaps even more generously than one who founds all his judgments of human conduct on the creed of some theistic religion. It may be that the rationalist finds it easier to pity human error and to deny the natural impulse to call it wickedness.

There is another pitfall here, however, which I think we must step by very carefully. If it is true that a valid ethical judgment may be immoral, and I think it may well be, since it may reject mere conformity to tribal rules, must it also be the result of an inner struggle? It is obvious that a truly ethical person would prefer to conform if possible to the rules of his tribe, since he prefers decency and courtesy to mere eccentricity. In that sense, an ethical judgment which went against conventional morality would be the result of a struggle between ordinary good manners and inner conviction. But must the true ethical judgment come from a conflict of the spirit? Or can it be the serene and calm decision of a clear insight into the situation? Must one struggle against inner evils to be sure of being fit to confront evils outside?

What we are dealing with here, with brutal simplicity perhaps, is the old question of the man who finds it easy to be good. Is he a good man?

The rationalist is inclined, I think, Montaigne to the contrary notwithstanding, to reject a question of this sort as logomachy. He does not believe that the rightness of an action can be accidental; he does not call an action good because of its practical results when it was taken with an intention to commit an evil. He is perhaps legalistic enough to think that an action is good if it was intended to do good, and results in good, whether or not it required self-sacrifice on the part of the actor. And if an act is good, in these circumstances, then an ethical judgment may be valid if it is purely intellectual, entailing no humility or suffering on the part of the person who makes it. Ethical success does not require travail of the spirit. The rationalist may recognize such travail as part of the human condition and as good spiritual exercise, but will not confuse this with ethical judgment. Indeed, the rationalist may be suspicious of judgments arrived at with too much inner suffering because he knows that the logical powers are not purified by pain, even though courage and dedication may be.

Ethical success then is not merely living a prudentially good life. It is also not conquest of evil motives in one's self. A rationalist ethic requires a clear idea of both these elements in life, however, and a man who undertakes to live by ethical judgments must take them into account, just as he takes into account other less directly pertinent facts in his condition, such as physical pain and pleasure, failure and success in material affairs, and life's simple ultimates in love and work and rest. An ethical judgment is an attempt to decide how one is to manage all these elements and the accidental factors in the challenging situation in order to attain the greatest possible good.

If the good is not defined by revelation, nor by custom, how is it defined? By what ethical right do I accept the definition of the English philosopher I quoted in the beginning? Is the rationalist merely setting up his own logic against the wisdom of others, as the growing child may rebel against the rules by which he is being made into a human being fit to live in a certain time and place? The utilitarians of the early nineteenth century faced this problem with courage. Whatever we may think of their success, we have to see a sublime faith in reason in the effort to push the doctrine of the greatest good (meaning pleasure) of the greatest number to the point of saying that any man's idea of the good is equal to that of any other man. Their rule was, in fact, no rule at all and their ethics were an abdication from which they were saved only by their inconsistencies.

We are compelled to reject the simplistic formulas of utilitarianism by the fact that to say that one man's judgment of what is good will do as well as any other man's, is ultimately to have no standard of good whatever. There is, however, in the utilitarian creed a thread of truth which can be salvaged. If this were not true it would be difficult to understand how men of such powerful minds as Jeremy Bentham and the two Mills, father and son, could have accepted it. The thread of truth is in its altruism, its basic search for the basic good in the welfare of others, not the self.

The truth is there in part but it needs much more explication. Merely to say that we devote ourselves to the good of others is not much more satisfactory than to say that we devote ourselves wholly to the development of our best selves. The first of these two oversimple views is the essence of the Stoic doctrine which can be called, I suppose, the rationalism of the ancients. In the break up of the Greek political system, in a world which seemed to offer no career of happy usefulness to anyone, there were two philosophical systems which appealed to the practical imagination of the Greeks. The Platonic and Aristotelian systems blazed out like the fire on the funeral pyre of their culture and they were too demanding for the times. But a man could retreat from an impossible world, which was the course taught by the Epicureans as the way to quiet happiness, or he could face duty without hope of happiness, disdaining in fact all but the sense of self-respect. The Stoic half of this pessimism was a kind of rationalism, and it was altruistic in one sense. The Stoic lived for duty; that was a way of living for others. But he loved nobody, not even himself. And not loving either others or himself he missed the deepest spiritual meaning of altruism, which is to realize not our duty but our happiness in service to others. Stoicism was founded by Zeno who is supposed to have been a Semite and this is curious, because what Stoicism lacks is just that element of love for one's brother which came into European thought in the Judeo-Christian teachings and flowered in Christianity.

This gives us, I think, another way of putting our definition of the good, and also a way of describing ethical success whether it is sought by moral rules, religious teachings, or rational thought. It is to find happiness in the welfare of others. This has to be distinguished, of course, from the possessive demand that someone else find his happiness according to our choices rather than by his own. The rationalist thinks he is as likely to escape that sin of self-righteousness as is the next man. And one of the greatest of all rationalists, David Hume, taught one of our two principles of rational faith, the natural sociability and gregariousness of man.

It would have to be a basic principle with any rationalist, I believe, that his system of ethics would lead him to much the same ethical judgments in practical morality as would be arrived at by the religious paths that have been expounded in this series. He would not expect to differ from Protestant, or Catholic, or Jew, or any other devout man in serving justice or mercy or charity; he would not expect to differ, but if he did he would not be dismayed. He would seek a reasonable agreement. Above all, the rationalist is a believer in what I have elsewhere called spiritual democracy. He asks that in the work of the world men do what they can together in harmony without demanding agreement on ultimate sanctions. If Protestant or Catholic or Jew, whatever he himself may be, will cooperate in furthering the agreed on welfare of men, he will ask no questions.

In the announcements of this series you were promised that we would stand up to be counted on some issues of public and domestic concern. The other men have been here as spokesmen for definite creeds; I have been speaking for the possibility of ethical principles that were not founded on any creed, although I have insisted that they are not in conflict with any religious belief which was not in itself unethical.

Beginning with the self and the most intimate personal relations, we can go outward to show how this works in the broadest of human affairs. What about family life? The rationalist would answer that question by asking another. What is a family for? And if someone should reply that a family is for the glory of God, he would have to reply that this is only another way of naming the problem. A family is for the welfare of its members on this earth, the development of healthy and if possible happy individuals, to the fullest extent of their endowment. It may have other purposes but they cannot, in reason, be in conflict with this. Such success cannot be achieved unless there is firm moral teaching or, to put it in naturalistic terms, a clear initiation into the ways of the tribe. The child has to live in a certain time and place; he must know the rules, what is expected of him, what he will be held accountable for, what goals are permitted and what denied. The minute terms of these moral teachings are not ethical questions. They are customary. That is reason enough. It is necessary also, in our society, that the basic moral teaching include the education which will make it possible for the child to understand freedom and live by freedom. At this task we have not done too well but the rationalist would say that we would do better if we put more reason into our methods, not more coercion or more precept.

A home is bound together by the respect of every member for every other. This is the most intimate expression of the simple loyalty of one human being to others. If it can be warmed by affection and good humor and pleasant ways, so much the better. The rationalist knows the power of love and he hopes for its blessing. But he wants it to be free of possessiveness and informed by patient knowledge.

If a home is thus marked by freedom and respect it cannot be a place that breeds selfishness and it may make demands for heavy sacrifice. It happens sometimes that self-sacrifice is necessary if the welfare of one is identified with the welfare of all, and it is reasonable to see that one of the great ways of realizing one's self is in paying heavily for the chance of another to realize himself. Parents and teachers, relatives and older friends all know this; it is one of the glories of commonplace lives. Does this give any guidance in such questions as the right or wrong of divorce, of intermarriage between members of different religious faiths, of the limitation of families? The rationalist is inclined to think that it is the only kind of thinking that does give any guidance in these matters and that the teachings of specific religious faiths on such questions get their strength and persuasiveness from their adherence to rational principles. He demands over and over again, whenever a question is asked in such matters, *cui bono?* For whose benefit? It is this question, not the citation of a rule in a book, that will clarify the issues in a tangle of emotion and fear and regret and shame and cowardice and cruelty, when the future of a family is at stake. A divorce, for whose benefit? A calculus of goods, in the fashion of the Utilitarian philosophers may be absurd, but there is a practical compelling usefulness in looking at any such question from the standpoint, in turn, of every member of the family and of every person likely in any way to be affected. An interfaith marriage? A family too large for the material and spiritual income of the parents? For *whose* good?

What I am saying, of course, is that there are no rules, in reason, to settle such matters; there is only experience, the judgment of the wise, and the brave thinking of those involved. The young have to be counselled, but what good is counselling unless it is based on reason? I am also saying that the rationalist would try to make all important "ought" questions into questions of ethics, not of morals. As I have made the arbitrary distinction, morals have to do with the rules of the group; they can sometimes be interpreted in different ways but generally they give answers, not guidance. If problems of conduct are settled by moral rules, enforced by religious sanctions, the answers may be good, they are not ethically speaking either good or bad. They are simply moral. If it should happen that reason suggests one answer and the moral rules give another, then the dilemma is real. Reason does not answer this kind of question. It only counsels the divided conscience to weigh carefully the values of moral compliance against the values of free choice. Both sets of values are real and in grave matters the loss of either one is damaging for life. But freedom is not easy and reason does not make for quiet happiness. Both reason and moral rule urge against selfishness or recklessness or wilful independence. The considered decision will be a test of ultimate character and no one can answer for the individual's conscience.

The principle works in the same way as we go outward from these more intimate concerns into social relations. A very good example would be the ethical meaning of the conflicts now going on in some of our Southern communities where long established social advantages are being divided among new claimants and where a way of life is being destroyed by the movement of humane progress. The way of life which is threatened by admitting Negro children to the schools that have been heretofore reserved for white children can properly be called a system of morals, although it is evil by any religious or ethical standard. There have been sincere men, and many of them, who have invoked religious principles for defending it. It was a form of social order. But the need to break it up was so great that the President of the United States had to call out armed men to enforce the orders of a Federal court. The rationalist's ethical approach to this problem would be to ask a question in terms of Thomas Hill Green's standard. Does discrimination help toward the ideal of making the "welfare of all the welfare of each"?

In questions like these it is not difficult to locate the bearing of rational principles on practical conduct. Difficulties increase when we get into broader areas. Is there, for example, any ethical meaning in the conflict between private and public initiative in economic affairs? Socialists have often based their arguments on what they said were ethical principles, and even on religious teaching. Since most of the great religions began historically as the cult of a small group of the founder's followers, and it was natural for the members of such a group to have all things in common, many men have convinced themselves that private possessions are somehow irreligious if not intrinsically evil. And elaborate scholarship in both

Germany and England, in Max Weber and R. H. Tawney, has set up the theory that modern capitalism was developed out of the usury which the medieval church abhorred. (It should be noticed that this abhorrence did not keep pious Catholics of the Middle Ages from condemning Jews to this sin for the public convenience.) To me the story seems a little forced. There could be no capitalism until there was a sufficient development of modern technology to make the use of fixed capital in the form of machinery profitable. In the nineteenth century it was as much the growth of modern forms of fiscal investment at it was the awakening of the public conscience that bettered working conditions in the factories. Ideas and conditions, as Whitehead has made clear in *The Adventures of Ideas,* have to work together if man's ethical judgments get established in institutions.

A rationalist is inclined to say that there is no ethical question involved in the conflict between two forms of organization, but that in the practice of any form there are always conflicts between personal and social interests. It is an ethical question for a man working in any economic system, no matter what, to decide how he is to balance his obligations to his family and himself against his opportunities to serve the larger welfare. And again we see that the rationalist tends to say that a mere moral, or conventional, or institutional judgment by rule will often fail to settle the question. He often insists we have to make the moral issue an ethical one, to get it out of the system of rules and make it a matter of conscious choice. He believes that men grow by choice, and learn by consequences, and that nothing done by unexamined rules counts in ethical experience. As we have said, many things are trivial by nature and most economic questions are of this kind. They should be relegated to moral rules in order to free the mind for the experience of choosing in greater areas of responsibility.

The extension of this principle to international affairs does not change the principle but the difficulties are greater. What are the moral—we would say, ethical—limits of the will to national survival? The rationalist would like to believe that here, too, he can rely on reason. To whose benefit should there be a United States of America? Are we quite sure that this country exists, as it is now, as it is likely to be in the time of our children, for the good of the people in it? I think the answer would be yes, but no one should shrink from asking himself the question. It is on the unthinking and merely emotional answer to that question that tyrants can always count if they want to suppress freedom in the name of safety, or send men to death.

Is the existence of the United States a good to the rest of the world? Only if it can be proved so, by reason. Most of our efforts in international affairs, beyond the mere animal necessity of protection against brutality, should be toward the end of making it possible for what is reasonable in our own country's spirit and policy to prove its worth by honest argument and consistent action.

Something remains to be said about the guidance which reason can give in one's attitude toward one's self. One of the great insights of modern psychology is that condemnation of self, or the feeling of guilt, is often irrational even if not neurotic, and that it has very little logical relation to actual conduct. It is not the most wicked in action who feel the heaviest guilt. This guilt feeling is not the healthful and restorative penitence which almost all religions have taught. It is not a source of energy for doing better, but an erosion of the will.

At this point, I think, there is more difficulty and possible conflict between the rational point of view and the religious than anywhere else in ethical thinking. I would insist that here as elsewhere a rational system can exist without a dogmatic commitment and that a dogmatic commitment can make good use of rational insights. But it is central to religious thinking that the fate of an individual soul is a drama of great significance and that God's interest in the person lifts his will to a level of momentous choice. We are "great" sinners, not insignificant ones. In almost a contradiction of this, the rational and scientific attitude toward man's behavior is that his conduct has much less meaning in the lives of others, and even in his own than he is likely to think. This is not to lessen our horrified realization that a stupid and ignorant person, even if not wicked in his will, may cause great misery to others. It is rather to insist that the ethical meaning of these cruel mistakes is small because the level of awareness was low and the choice made was trivial and for trivial reasons.

This lands us, I fear, in subtleties of casuistry into which we should hesitate to venture. But we are required to take note of the difficulties because here a rational ethics must challenge not only some kinds of religious beliefs but also the basic morals of Western civilization as embedded in the Common Law. The law, taking it briefly to begin with, defines responsibility thus: if one intends an act, he intends and is guilty of the consequences which could reasonably be expected to follow from that act.[4] He does not need to have explicit visions of these consequences, if he pushes a brick out of an upper story window he cannot say he didn't mean it if the brick hits someone on the head. The rational philosopher admits, of course, that such a principle may be quite necessary in morals, and in the administration of practical justice but would have to say also that it is essentially absurd. If we are really to be held for the consequences of every act we commit with full intention, anyone of us may be held guilty of much of the misery and cruelty in the world, not only now but forever after, since the nexus of cause and effect is a web of connections without disjunction. The effect of any act is incalculable and the enforcement of the Common Law is only a surface intervention at the level of commonplace connections and ostensible events. Were the art critics who poisoned the soul of Adolf Hitler by telling him that he could not paint, the responsible cause of Buchenwald? The rationalist finds it more reasonable to see man in his relative proportions and he may even believe, as I do, that a man may as likely draw back from wickedness because he sees it as foolish as to draw back because he smells brimstone.

I am saying that one can learn to regard his own behavior as "typical" and gain sanity thereby. And if neither religious scruples nor a sense of dignity keeps a man from an evil act, can he then

[4] *Cf.* Holmes, O. W. Jr., *The Common Law*, Little, Brown and Company, Boston, 1881, Chap. Three.

regain his self-respect after this and his chance at decent normal living by reason alone? Can he forgive himself?

The rationalist may claim that the idea of forgiving one's self is one of the ideas which rational ethical thinking has brought into the world. It is psychological insight, not a religious principle, that we cannot easily forgive others unless we have learned to forgive ourselves. And it is a typical scientific insight because it shows us that we are really brothers of all other men, neither so much better nor so much worse as we may, in dramatic imagination, picture ourselves. Does this so reduce a man's idea of his self that he loses the desire for good? There may be, as I say, a difficulty here and a possible conflict with much religious thinking. The rationalist falls back upon his principle of moderation. It is the excess of penitence which he thinks is dangerous to future conduct, the lashings of the soul which may satisfy some primitive instinct but which do not cleanse or release or prepare for future good. If seeing one's own sin in its due insignificance will help anyone to escape this kind of repentance, the rational thinker would say that there has been a great gain and that the future is more assured.

But is this relaxation dangerous in another way? Will the kind of healthy sanity which makes a man see his own actions in their due proportions take away the strong incentive to righteousness which a frightened conscience might provide? On this, again, we can only compare impressions; history is read in almost as many different fashions as it is written. It amounts to asking whether or not the present age, which is, we are told, heavily dominated by secular interests, is an evil time or comparatively a good one. And we know from repeated experience that there will be some who cry out that it is an evil time, because there are always men who say that and believe it. Insofar as their dissatisfaction is a way of stating their conviction that the times are too much invaded with wickedness, we can all agree. All times have been evil, when seen honestly by contemporaries or honestly reported. I have already recorded my belief that we get better not worse in human history.

The simplest way to state the rational case on this question of motive is to go back to Socrates who said that all men seek the good and those men who chose evil had made mistakes. He believed, and Plato seems to have believed with him for a long time, until the dissolution of Greek rationalism broke his heart and he turned to the sternness and dark pessimism of the Laws, that knowledge leads to good action. It must be noted that Socrates was not interested in physical science; he wanted men to apply their reason to such questions as we are here discussing—the nature of justice and the good, the true, and the beautiful, to the search for temperance and wisdom. If we have learned anything in ethics since the time of Socrates with the help of his pupils, I would say that it is what I have been insisting on here, that all knowledge helps toward the good. All knowledge of nature (*sive Deus*) whether of the inanimate energies of conscienceless matter or of ourselves as sentient mechanisms, helps us toward the good. Knowledge can be perverted: so can religious teaching. Its free effect, its social effect, is to increase what Green called the betterment of man in the "arts that make nature, both as used and as contemplated, the friend of man."

Rational ethics involve one's behavior toward other men, both inner and actual and one's attitudes and actions in behalf of institutions, ideals, and human purposes. One's behavior toward God, is not, strictly speaking, involved, except insofar as one's religious principles would lead him to say that God is served by this kind of secular righteousness. Rational ethics must specifically reject as satisfactory human behavior that kind of dedication to personal salvation which is recorded in such ancient books as the Golden Legend. Perhaps one will remember the story of the "saint" who left home to seek his salvation and told his parents nothing of what was happening to him. Then after years of ascetic effort he returned home and lived in his own house with his parents as a nameless beggar and never let them know that he was their long mourned son. To what purpose? is a fair question to the rationalist who does not see a conflict between righteousness or an honest search for knowledge and grace, and the ordinary devotions of natural life. If he is told that the beggar-son was a saint because he cherished the good of his own soul more than he did the love of father and mother, the rationalist can only recall the Fifth Commandment with a feeling that the old Hebrews were more humane if not more godly than the Christians of the Middle Ages. The logic of fanaticism is often impenetrable; is it sane?

The fair question to direct at my general thesis, that knowledge leads to righteousness, can be stated thus: Have we any reasons to believe that modern knowledge of the nature of man, scientifically arrived at, makes for better human relations? One could, of course, get bogged down here in trying to define good human relations; this discussion goes along a path beside endless quicksands of that kind. I mean by "good" those relations which lead to peace and kindness and the full rich development of every being. The rationalist is aware that there are some who would say that these virtues are irrelevant to salvation and immortal blessedness. He can only answer that such a judgment is outside the competence of the criteria he is going by and that what he seeks is peace on earth, goodwill to men.

The treatment of children by their parents is as good a field as any for a discussion of this point. Has scientifically acquired knowledge improved the relations between parents and children? My answer would be yes, beyond question, wherever it has been used. It is necessary, over and over, to insist that the existence of a large body of psychological knowledge, generally accessible, does not insure that it is used. It may be true that children today are less tractable and industrious than they used to be. The ethical philosopher who happens also to be a historian will remind us that they have always been intractable and lazy, by adult standards. If we are going to be reasonable in discussing the effect of reason on behavior we have to be scrupulously careful in choosing examples to show what we are talking about. And then we have to admit that even with all precautions we are talking largely about impressions; there are no records of manners and taste and standards among ordinary men, women, and children that are worth much, and memories are usually only our ideals of ourselves in reverse. We remember that "when we were young" things were different.

A little acquaintance with literature intended for children, such as Sunday School lessons, sermons, and such recorded expressions of the common pretended expectation, shows that judgments of childish behavior were almost wholly in terms of goodness and badness. Just as the insane were locked up in open cages to be jeered at for public amusement, so one suspects that sick little children were often whipped for being wicked. One wonders if most of the depravity of small minds and hearts was not what today we would call illness. Here again we have to be prepared to fend off those who "know" that there were no delinquents when they were young and that modern psychiatry and progressive education and all kinds of other demons have soured the soul of the modern child. And it may well be that wickedness, if there is such a thing, is often mistaken by a modern child psychologist for illness. But the furious child was certainly called wicked a hundred years ago.

We can trace three transformations away from this attitude. The first, in which many partly enlightened parents are still struggling, is to think of all strange conduct by their children as signs of illness. Does the little girl lie on the floor and scream for no reasons that she can explain or that you can guess? The first change away from calling her wicked or even possessed of a devil, is to say that she is sick. And, of course, it may be that she is. But parents who have gone a little further—but perhaps not yet far enough in their grasp of modern psychology—will transfer the concept of wickedness to themselves and ask, what did I do to bring this on?

This guilty attitude toward the ancient misbehaviors of a child is still common, of course, but it may stem as much from the attitude of the parent toward himself as from his attitude toward the child, and on that account it is not quite in the progression of changes. In former times, before we knew as much as we know now, in explicit terms, about such matters, a parent might well have had a strong feeling of guilt in meeting the disobedience of his child. But if he followed the convention of his age he would be likely to feel that he was neglecting the child by sparing the rod and instead of wondering what had been his own sin he would cure everything by administering a sound beating.

The most enlightened parent of today may greet the minor misbehaviors of his child with an interested "How typical of that age in these circumstances!" By doing so he certainly relaxes the tension in the situation. He also brings up the old question in its newest form. Is the recognition of a supposed typicality in the behavior of another a better response than to make a judgment?

Our first answer has to be, as indicated, that it is better certainly in one way; it makes for less bitterness and saves the child from reprisal. But does the child learn from it? That we would say at once depends on the parent? Is it a substitute for love? Perhaps. But it is a better substitute for love, one may believe, than is hatred.

This is not, I think, a mere modern version of the old adage which one usually quotes in French, *"Tout comprendre c'est tout pardonner,"* "To understand all is to pardon everything." It is rather expressed by saying that if we understand more we know better what is to be forgiven and what is really evil. I am insisting that knowledge, verifiable material knowledge, such as we might have of chemistry or physics, when we can gain it about ourselves and other human beings, makes us more sensitive to good and evil, not less. It makes us know what is a wilfully chosen evil, the only kind which even theologians recognize, and what is mistake or illness or frustration or mere growing pains.

The sins of childhood may be trivial but the relations between children and parents are central to ethical standards. They express the relation between the strong and the weak. They involve the problem of affection as a blind to wisdom. They are diurnal and irreversible. They have the greatest of all advantages in human experience in that we can see, if we are honest and watchful, at least some of the results of our own behavior and can learn.

I would not hesitate to generalize on my example. There are very few kinds of human interchange, none that I can think of, that would not be improved by better knowledge. Love is necessary, but even real love, which is not mere possessiveness or selfish identification, can make mistakes through ignorance. A good part of the world's misery up to now has been caused by mistakes of affection. The bruised bodies and broken hearts of millions of children through thousands of years are all the proof we need for that.

The rationalist should be as much aware of the natural perversity of men as is anyone else and he cannot fail to note that to be treated as typical instead of being punished as wicked may offend the dignity of some mature persons. The subtleties of the spirit that lead men into adding the sin of pride to their other sins when they are charged with wickedness, are too commonly observed to be denied and they are not yet fully explained. The delinquent boy who is told that we understand him, that we know he is only blowing off steam and expressing himself in the gang patterns which his culture offers him, may be offended because he is, in his own eyes, a romantic figure of loyalty to evil. His elders may in less obvious ways insist also on their right to be punished. In dealing with this kind of resistance the rationalist is baffled because it is itself essentially irrational. The rational, like all other methods of considering the world has limits. He would insist however that the method works to lessen tensions in most cases and that when we are dealing with irrational or perverse elements in human nature, knowledge is an advantage even when it is not deep enough to be adequate. We need more knowledge then, not a substitute for it.

This one example of perversity, however, brings up the whole program of objections to rational ethics which is urged by a prominent school of modern thinkers who have rediscovered with the aid of a few megalomaniacs in politics that there is irrationality in men and that an aseptically logical plan for human behavior is sure to be defeated by human nature's more darkly emotional side. This shows itself in the political writings of some thinkers who talk nonsense about the bankruptcy of science in human affairs, pretending that science in human affairs has been tried. It shows itself in some intellectuals of feeble wills and shaky imaginations who sentimentalize history and so reject modern man. On this basis obscurantism flourishes in religion and in literature, as well as in public affairs, and education is made nugatory.

The rationalist may be dismayed by this kind of pessimism, just as he has been dismayed by the revivals of hysterical wickedness which tyrants exploiting irrationalism can bring on. He is reminded of the fact that whenever in the past, as for example in the middle of the fourth century B.C., Western man has seemed at last to have reached a point of faith in his own reason, that brief illuminated time has been followed by an engulfing tide of mystery and darkness and superstition. A great modern scholar whose studies in the irrationality of the ancient world have helped us to understand our own world shows how the gap between the beliefs of the rational intellectuals of Greece and the delusion ridden common people in the fourth century was what did the tragic damage.[5] The rationalist of today may well wonder if the revolt against reason which is also the revolt against freedom is not latent in men, as in the opposite and constructive drive toward reason on which he counts, perhaps too confidently.

He is entitled to say, however, that rational ethics cannot be dismissed because they are too difficult, any more than a religious program can be dismissed as too stern for common men. The record of reason in producing humane and helpful behavior among men, when put against all the other records, will stand.

So much for applications. Theory, however, does not stand or fall by practical experience alone, any more than religious doctrines are judged wholly by their fruits. The principles are to be studied and debated as principles, as well as followed as guides to living. It is this examination that we have attempted here. The principles are an extension of the implications of our first quotation from T. H. Green. An ethical system, he said, should help us in the mastery of nature for our own purposes and further the brotherhood of man. Our two basic principles both contribute to both these purposes. The advancement of learning not only helps to control nature by the understanding of natural events; it also humanizes humanity. And the satisfaction of the learning urge in man, aids

[5] Dodds, E. R., *The Greeks and the Irrational*, Beacon Press, Boston, 1957.

him because he is naturally a social being and learning is one of the greatest and most profoundly effective of social enterprises. We get wisdom in order to get righteousness and the world is ultimately man's spiritual home.

VI

ETHICAL FRONTIERS

BY

WALTER G. MUELDER

Dean and Professor of Social Ethics Boston University School of Theology

In this essay I shall be concerned with two types of ethical frontiers as they relate to patterns of religious ethics. The first type relates to the internal frontier or the institutional dilemma of religious bodies as they undertake to effect social change. The second type relates to four selected frontiers in the social order outside the church as an institution. These four are the frontier of abundance, the frontier of the family, the frontier of mass communications, and the frontier of nuclear warfare. At the conclusion we shall return to the dilemma of responsibility that confronts the churches and other religious bodies.

Mankind's revolutionary predicaments present an exceedingly complex range of moral frontiers. These frontiers relate on the normative side to the universal ideals of churches, temples, and synagogues. They relate on the sociological side to the fact that mankind must be conceived as a unit of cooperation. In between these poles is the dilemmatic fact that religions and cultures with universal ideals are rooted in and accommodated to institutions and social systems which are limited in space, time, and function. At the same time these institutions and social systems are undergoing rapid social change. This social change on its technical side is consciously purposive. Social orders are being deliberately changed on a massive scale. Such changes mean that not only are the universal religions being related to each in a new way but their supporting cultures are purposively being changed and brought into conflict with each other.

I wish to lay particular stress on the fact that universal religions are being judged morally by their capacity to function universally at the very time that they are intensively accommodated to cultures which are in flux and in conflict. This observation lies behind my first consideration of the internal frontiers or institutional dilemmas.

I

Internal Frontiers: Institutional Dilemmas

The patterns of ethics which have been presented in this series as Judaism, Roman Catholicism, and Protestantism are, on the one hand, universal in ideals and, on the other hand, the theological ethics of a specialized religious body. These ideals are universal in form but not necessarily in function or effect. In practice they make a universal assertion and demand upon the world but do not seem to make a similar demand upon the churches within whose life the ethic is formulated.

Much contemporary theological ethics not only grounds itself in a revelation given only to the group or its founder, but specifically disclaims the authority of a more general revelation or natural moral law. When the general natural moral law is recognized, it is accorded a secondary and subordinate place. The primary and even ultimate status is accorded the theological claims of the particular religious body. In effect, this tends to mean social exclusiveness. What is common to all or even to several religions is given a lower status.

Judaism, Roman Catholicism, and Protestantism all claim to be universal religions but do not have corresponding institutional structures and functions. Their ideals are universal and their memberships are widely scattered, but they are not sociologically universal. This fact has significant ethical consequences. Indeed, the universal ideals which they profess (such as love, justice, mercy, peace, integrity, responsibility) may actually serve to blind the religious bodies to the fact that their societies function with restrictive practical goals. As conceptual systems of ideas they envisage universal communities, but as operational institutions they are culturally accommodated. Paradoxically, the more absolute and unique the claim, the more restrictive in practice the bodies tend to become. Universal ideals are used to sanction exclusive groups.

We may illustrate the dilemmas briefly. Judaism teaches ethical monotheism; it is a prophetic religion. Its ethical vision is inclusive. In practice, however, it often functions as the cultural, ethical, or religious pattern of a community whose life is oriented spiritually in the destiny of Israel. As a consequence in practical cultural matters and international affairs, the welfare of Israel often becomes a kind of criterion of international policies. Prophetic religion defines the moral frontier.

In the case of Roman Catholics we have an analogous dilemma. Here the tendency is to identify the kingdom of God on earth with the Church. Because of its theory of the divinely instituted hierarchy and papal authority no final tension between the kingdom of God and the Church in history is admitted. The Church operates, of course, as an accommodated organization adapted to various cultures, economic orders, and political systems. Its universal supernatural claims have formal consistency but little correlation with diverse operational patterns in national states except that they tend in every instance to be authoritarian.

The Roman Catholic pattern of ethics has the advantage of including the principle of natural law. According to this conception right reason in all persons can apprehend basic moral laws. Through such a natural law concept all nations should be able to participate in worldwide community for temporal ends without first submitting to the Church's authority over supernatural good. In fact, however, the natural moral law as used by the Church is given substantive content and interpretation drawn from tradition and revelation. Consequently the natural law does not function as a universal social principle. Both revealed and natural ethics become largely the functions of the Church and its interests.

The situation in Protestantism is equally dilemmatic. Since

Protestantism has not solved the problem of freedom in relation to unity and order, its universal ethical ideals are ineffectively related to social action. Denominationalism and sectarianism are the result of convictions freely accommodated to the middle classes and to the frustration and dissent of the lower classes. In some cases they reflect the apathy of social defeat and individual despair. Despite a growing ecumenical consciousness and the formulation of the ethical norm of "the responsible society," Protestantism is complacent beyond all protest. Moreover, its current sophisticated rejection of both natural law and philosophical ethics, together with its failure to wrestle with ethical casuistry, has prevented its formulating a common witness on world affairs. By this same theological fashion it has gone far toward destroying any method of communication with others.

The general tendencies to ground its ethics exclusively in faith, to find faith only in the church's fellowship, and to accommodate the church to the middle class tend to cut Protestantism off from effective cooperation with non-Christian groups except on an ad hoc, expedient, and transitory political basis. It lacks agreed upon "middle axioms," a confidence in any kind of natural moral law, and a body of responsible casuistry. Some denominations will, of course, disclaim this composite picture, but it represents an all too prevalent pattern.

Here then is an internal frontier, an institutional dilemma, which in different ways confronts the universalist religions. An ethical monotheism, a God of love, brings a demand for brotherliness on an operational level which is bound to conflict with the requirements of class, community, and national citizenship. At the very time when inclusive norms and values are imperatively required, there is a tendency on the part of religious institutions to transform them into images desired by the nurturing culture.

The task of the churches is to win the necessary autonomy, achieve self-awareness of their dilemmas, and develop the leadership necessary to make universal ideals concretely operative. No one can doubt the risks which the churches must take as institutions if they are to function as leaders in supra-national interdependence.

They must take the full measure of political and economic pressures which find their religious idealism a convenient instrument to be used for expedient ends. There is much unmasking to do, for lofty religious symbols often cloak interest-limited values.

The state has a stake in the harmony of social ideals which are allegedly present in the Judeo-Christian tradition. But the proper interest of the religious bodies in those same values is not the same as the state's. We must examine the nature and role of these values more closely.

Despite the diversity of interests at work in American society, there is an impressive complex of common social ideals which is actually quite pervasive. It is often asserted that a relatively homogeneous ethic is carried about in the blood stream of American society drawn from the language of the Judeo-Christian ethic. There is considerable evidence for this, though the term Judeo-Christian has lost its wartime popularity. Such is the relation of religion to culture that when powerful religious bodies emphasize common values, the integration of society is greatly advanced. The need for national unity during the war drew on all available common elements. Conversely, when creedal and ethical differences are emphasized by churches and temples in competition with each other, the tensions in society are increased.

This American situation has its effect on the world scene. At once it becomes apparent that a much wider range of religious systems is involved. The predominant religions of the Bandung community, for example, are not those of the Judeo-Christian community, though the latter are not entirely absent. If the world community is to be developed, it is imperative that common values be stressed by all the living world religions, or else that they abdicate their role as integrators of society in favor of some secular substitute. The requirement would be that their supra-national or universalist values be effectively emphasized despite resultant conflict with nationalist political demands. Should this development fail by default and the growing self-consciousness of national cultures increase, the creedal differences in the religious systems will be exploited to accentuate tension in world society. We would then have the anomaly of universalist religions promoting the destruction of world brotherhood. Each of the world religions was once the creator of a culture. Can they transcend their cultures and create world community?

How are we to arrive at those common values in the internal frontiers of our religious institutions? In the American scene they have come to the fore through a common heritage and the socialization of competing groups in a democratic society. Secular groups and interests, lay people in public schools, industry, and politics became aware of the practical similarity of social ideals implicit in the various religious bodies and, through persistent expectation, called out a common expression of behavior even when such was not the logical product of the diverse sectarian beliefs. Social interaction in a free society stimulated awareness of common social goals in the various expressions of theological ethics. These goals comprise the "American Dream"; and most Americans believe them to be a rationally defensible set of values, rooted in the dignity of the person. These values give coherence to our social existence.

I should like to suggest that on the world level it is important to explore those common human values which give all participants in the world community a sense of belonging to a common world community. These common values must be institutionalized in world bodies or recognized to be operative in agencies already in existence. To be operationally effective these values must be not only those of leaders who pronounce generalizations, but of the broad membership who will acknowledge the values in worship, education, and action.

There is a real question in my mind whether the religious bodies of the living world religions are prepared to embrace the moral and anthropological conceptions which are presupposed in any conversation across cultural boundaries. By such conceptions I mean the general view that the nature of man, in spite of all differences, is the same in all cultures, races, and periods of history; that the same laws describe him not only physiologically, but psychologically and socially; and that certain values and aims of his self-realization follow from his nature. I do not expect that all religions would provide the same ultimate explanations of his common nature or invoke the same ultimate sanctions for his conduct.

Are the various religions of mankind going to ignore these aspects of the created world which are open to rational and empirical reflection and to insist on transforming their distinctive and conflicting doctrines of salvation into competing prior dogmas of anthropology despite such evidence?

These issues point to the internal frontier, or institutional dilemmas, of all universalist religious institutions.

II

External Frontiers: Dilemmas of Transformation

In the revolutionary world situation the ethical frontiers run the whole extent of the cultural spectrum from the family to the international political community. I shall refer briefly to four clusters of new issues which challenge traditional patterns of social ethics. All of these have implications for and are involved in the unity of mankind. These four are: (1) the frontier of productive abundance; (2) the frontier of family life; (3) the frontier of mass communications; and (4) the frontier in nuclear warfare.

A. *The Frontier of Productive Abundance.* This frontier is the product of technology and social organization. The possibility of a worldwide abundance has aroused all nations to pursue the new technology and to explore various new types of social organization. Each nation seeks to raise its standard of living through industrialization and agricultural transformation. This means that the ethical ideas of freedom and justice, for example, are being filled with assignments in productivity looking toward abundance. It means that in the United States some are perplexed by the problem of how "to survive sanely and morally in the midst of the orgy of goods."

The new situation challenges, in either case, the older ideas of distributive justice which emphasized equity in the distribution of scarce goods by emphasizing a responsible development of an adequate production of goods. Thus far the world religions have had greater effect on the ethics of distribution than on production. Many unforeseen problems arise when one seeks not only a just division of an existing pie which is too small but even more the baking of an adequate pie. Where abundance is a possibility, poverty is an especially mortal sin. Since the rate of creating abundance is so uneven in the world we have the particularly perplexing dilemma of learning how to live with it at home and learning how to help achieve it soundly abroad.

There is no doubt that the concentration on abundance at home —even in minimal welfare terms—challenges the old religiously rooted values of renunciation, self-denial, and poverty. High consumption affects the morality of thrift and saving and the attitude toward the passing day. If sensuality is the inordinate love of transient good, then sensuality has become a major vice of American consumers. This type of sin challenges the nation to an effective education in values suitable to a responsible democracy. Indulgence in a high rate of vulgar consumption has the additional effect of creating widespread complacency toward all burning issues, including a sense of irresponsibility toward those parts of the world that are hopelessly frustrated by unspeakable scarcity.

It is not too early to be concerned about the gospel of higher and higher levels of consumption at earlier and earlier stages of family life. It is not too early to consider the national profile of longer vacations, longer weekends, more holidays and the attendant transformation of the gospel and discipline of work into a vulgar hedonism of comfort, security, and bodily excitement. But an even more urgent problem is the question of who or what will guarantee the rate of income needed to sustain personal and family spending at the high rate now becoming habitual. This issue has important bearings on the economics of longevity, retirement, and welfare for older persons. Who is responsible, the family or the community? If both, in what proportions? Shall the responsibility for abundant production be left to private enterprise primarily while the responsibility for equitable distribution, security, and welfare are assigned primarily to government? What is a sound pattern of responsibility?

While we are wrestling with the social ethics of abundance at home, we are challenged to even more radical thoughts on the international economic and political aspects of abundance. Give-away schemes have limited usefulness. Sharing is a virtue, but it does not automatically illuminate the questions of how much, to whom, when, what kind, and for what ends? In a world where technical change so profoundly affects cultural patterns, responsible giving and responsible receiving must be integrally conceived. In such a world bilateral arrangements may upset the balances of sound multilateral agreements. There is probably no area of life which is more crucial for the stability and development of human welfare than that of the right motivation and the intelligent management of international trade. Here is perhaps the major challenge to the re-education of the peoples of the world.

B. *The Frontier of Family Life.* Technical advances, high levels of employment, education, and woman's freedom to express herself in every phase of culture have developed a profound crisis in family life. The family has become vulnerable to an unprecedented degree.

When cries of family crisis are raised, some defenders point to the improvement of family living as indicated by the rapid development of the suburbs, the one-family houses, the earlier marriages, the larger number of children, the family television set, the revived interest in church activities, and the like. These are important data. There is, despite these developments, an ethical frontier in family life. It means that basic decisions are required which bear on the quality of the family bond, relations of the marriage partners to each other, and the role of the family in the nurture of children in responsible economic and political life.

The economic freedom of women, the labor-saving devices in housekeeping and cooking, and the family security provided by the community have removed many of the older family bonds and have, therefore, placed the greatest stress on the individual adjustment of the marriage partners to each other. For these reasons the psychological and spiritual bonds—the qualitative ones of personal respect, compatibility, and motivation for marriage—have to bear the strains of modern life. Individualistic or egocentric goals on the part of either partner make the marriage relationship highly vulnerable.

This vulnerability of the psychological bond is accentuated by the new tensions that develop on a massive scale because of the large number of working wives and mothers. There are many issues here, but I should like to select one for special emphasis. It is the relationship between the functional status system of the work-a-day world and the mutuality-status system of the family order. Men and women have always played complementary roles. Increasingly they are playing competing roles. These roles affect status in the world of work outside the home and increasingly affect status in the family itself. Since the roles we play influence the profiles of our characters, a study of these has a bearing on the ethics of family life.

Formerly, in the one-income family, the husband confronted two orders of status in which he alternated, one from 7 a.m. to 5 p.m. and the other from 5 p.m. to 7 a.m. On his job his status was measured by his efficiency. He was constantly confronted by the challenge to measure up to objective performance expectations or lose whatever standing he had with his associates who were also his competitors. At 5 p.m. he went home to his family, to relaxation, renewal, and rest. He left the order of competition to enter the order of mutuality. In the family he *had* his status born not of efficiency but of love. Here was emotional security, the wife knowing her role in a complementary society of primary acceptance, and accepting this role in maintaining the traditional values of home life. The family was thus a solidarity group within which status, rights, and obligations were defined in terms of membership as such, and by differences in age, sex, and biological relatedness. As Talcott Parsons and others have so clearly shown, this basis of relationship and status in the family precludes any major emphasis on standards of functional performance such as are typical in work situations away from home.

When both husband and wife work outside the home they tend to bring to the most intimate relationships of family life the ethos of the occupational world. In so doing they put the psychological bonds of the marital ties to the greatest test, apart from sheer disloyalty. As we have said, status and function are closely correlated in the occupational world. This relationship stresses competition in performance and achievement. Within the family the solidarity of life must be protected against the kinds of tensions that accompany severe competition for status between the members. This protection was provided when occupational role and family role were clearly separate from each other. However, when the marriage partners are proving themselves from evening to morning in relation to each other and the children, after having competed with others all day in the occupational world, they are caught in a never-ending round of insecurity and anxiety.

In the love of true marriage and family life the aggressive tendencies of each partner are reversed and the "thou" of the other overshadows the "ego" of the self. Consequently, when both marriage partners work outside the home, there is a danger that occupational patterns of function and status will undermine the basis of family solidarity. This threat may be all the more acute in those homes where the woman's achievement in the occupational world is conspicuously more successful than the man's. She may injure both his self-respect and his formal status with the further result of diminishing the emotional support she offers to her husband. The tensions of conflicting roles, even when the working wife is not competitive or aggressive within the home, create difficulties for her. The two roles—and there may be several—create a dilemma. On the one hand, she is supposed to be full of drive, self-assertion, competitiveness, and aggression—an achiever; on the other hand, her role calls for a relaxation of these assertive requirements, and more stress on efforts to please, on protecting or nurturing, on passivity and receptivity.

When conflict between these two sets of values is not resolved by right motivation, understanding, acceptance, education, and love the family is endangered. For both men and women in our culture at the present time this aspect of family life constitutes a major frontier. What is at stake is not the right of women to work outside the home. What is at stake is the meaning of family life itself.

C. *The Mass Communications Frontier.* A third ethical frontier of contemporary culture is in mass communications. Like the economy of abundance and the dilemmas of family roles, it has been created by basic achievements in technology and social organization. How important are mass communication media? It is easy both to overestimate and to underrate them. The means of communication, in any case, deeply influence the spiritual life of man, the quality of his choices and appreciations, the going standards of valuation, and the character of democratic action in politics. Mass communications, over a long period of time, may prove to have more influence on the spirit of man than the improvement of social and economic standards of production and consumption. This power is due to its all-pervasive character, bathing the mind and emotions in a continuous sea of images, sounds, signs, and meanings, but its methods are controlled increasingly by bigness and centralization which characterize so much of our practical and economic existence.

Recent studies lift up two kinds of basic moral questions with respect to the above situation. First, how can the freedom of the person and the vitality of culture be conserved and yet the whole community be served with information and entertainment? Secondly, how can personal responsibility in decision-making be enhanced in the use and organization of mass media of communication? These questions are too large to be disposed of adequately here, but certain facets of their challenges can be underscored.

The development of television has intensified the aggressiveness of advertising and has invaded the privacy of the home and the viewer as newspapers never could. What are the respective rights of the listener and viewer and of the advertiser, and what are the ethical limitations upon the broadcaster? When television and the movie producers combine to play directly before livingroom audiences—taking much of the time formerly devoted to movie-going in addition to the hours already devoted to TV—the personality and character-shaping power of this medium of communication will be even greater. Naturally this developing situation raises the question how the quality of personal integrity is to be conserved.

There is the closely related problem of balancing the claims of personal privacy and the right of the public to know. When the press, radio, and television attend a legislative hearing or investigation there are the conflicting claims of the public and the rights of accused persons to a fair trial since details shared with the public may tend to prejudice the verdict. In other situations there are the competing values of a completely libertarian policy in radio and television over against some degree of control by government.

These moral problems are especially complex because they are lock-stitched into the whole fabric of the social order. A man once asked, "Why do so many newspapers take the viewpoint of big business?" The reply was, "Because newspapers *are* big business." The same response belongs to all the major institutions which are developing the mass media of communication. What rights do stations and advertisers have in slanting the news to favor their interests? How can we be protected from both manipulation and conformism? Who have responsibilities in these matters?

A recent study by Wilbur Schramm shows that there are essentially two basic philosophies of mass communication, the libertarian and the authoritarian. The older authoritarian pattern has a special subtype, the Soviet control system. The older libertarian philosophy has as a modern subtype what may be called the concept of social responsibility. If the classical libertarian view had as its backdrop the authoritarian patterns of state and church, the newer social responsibility philosophy of freedom has as its backdrop the Soviet pattern of authority.

It is difficult to formulate a satisfactory and workable policy, but certain goals may set the sights for ethical deliberation: (a) keeping alive in persons and the public a critical and creative response to what is seen and heard; (b) providing means for the expression of free and independent response; (c) providing access to relevant facts and conflicting opinions and interpretations; (d) raising social conflict from the plane of violence to the plane of discussion; (e) insuring the rights of minorities to be heard; (f) clarifying the distinction between reasonable governmental intervention and a governmental monopoly that uses the media as an instrument of social policy; (g) clarifying the distinction between a negative kind of freedom based on liberty from external control and one that is positively devoted to the enhancement of personality. Cutting across a number of these goals is the difficulty of gratifying the desire of many to broadcast or print their opinions in view of the scarcity of channels and the expensiveness of setting up a newspaper office, or a radio, or television station and providing programs. These are a few of the issues on the frontier of social responsibility as it affects the opportunities for men and women to communicate with each other.

D. *The Frontier of Nuclear Weapons.* The final frontier which must be taken account of is in the development of sound national and international policies for the use and control of nuclear energy. Testing nuclear weapons may be used as a specific instance.

Man's immemorial dilemmas regarding militarism and military defense are intensified by the vast destructiveness of nuclear weapons, by the involvement of civilians on a gigantic scale, by the threats of increasing and cumulative radiation and their effects on generations yet unborn, and by the lethal effect of tests on innocent persons and unborn children in places far removed from the test sites. In addition to these problems are the mounting evidences of an arms race which steps up the conflicts among nations to unprecedented proportions.

In the arms race national pride and hysterical fear combine to threaten the balances in all levels of education. Natural science and technology may undermine curriculum developments in the humanities and social science. These are the disciplines whose weakness has exacerbated the international conflict. The dysfunctions incident to an imbalance of natural science and technology increases the influence of the military sectors of society to the detriment of democracy.

Our initial response must be that just as the civilian side of government must maintain its clear dominance over military power and organization, so in the total educational effort spiritual, social, and moral disciplines must be dominant over natural science and technology. If the battle against poverty and disease is to be won the sciences must be encouraged, but if the battle against tyranny and exploitation is to be won, the moral and behavioral sciences must be given a leading position in higher education.

If there is to be any worthy future for mankind that future must be spiritually and morally grounded. There is a moral difference between the Communist organization of society and its procedures and those of the "free world." This moral difference resides not only in the diverse ends which are pursued, but even more basically in the relating of means to ends; for the ends are predetermined in the means. Methods determine outcomes. Is it not one of the greatest condemnations of the Soviet system that it holds to an ethic which says that for an alleged good end "anything" is allowed? This resort to "anything" necessary may mean repudiation of the pledged word, slave labor camps, liquidation of farmers, violent purges of political opponents, and many other forms of ruthless expediency. The goal allegedly is the classless society; the means are dictatorship by the party and ruthless suppression of opposition.

Having said this of the Soviet Union must we not also say that it would be immoral for *any* nation to adopt the maxim: for an alleged good end "anything" is allowed? Furthermore, must we not say that in nuclear weapons of the kind now being tested and envisaged we have a means which makes possible the ultimate in human destruction? If this be the case are we not in the moral dilemma of embracing the ethics of current Communism: for an alleged good end (the defense of the nation or the Western world) anything is allowed?

If, then, it is wrong to engage in nuclear warfare, it follows that we are not justified in making nuclear weapons tests. To us belongs the moral challenge—moral, not expedient—of finding other ways to communicate a fundamental sense of responsibility for peace, freedom, and justice among nations. This is our moral frontier—with no guarantees of what lies beyond—except the universality of human nature, its needs and aspirations, and our capacity to help satisfy them in terms that respect the dignity of underdeveloped nations.

The moral challenge to the churches, temples, and synagogues is of unprecedented seriousness. Are they willing to risk what is necessary to make the judgment on nuclear weapons which is required if the nation is to make the judgment which the world is clearly yearning for? Our religious bodies can make their major impact on social change and process when they assert their spiritual and moral (and when necessary their material) autonomy in society. In making strategic decisions religious bodies must be fully aware of the social dilemmas in their accommodation to state and community; they must rediscover their prophetic leadership in thousands of churches—not only at national headquarters; and they must be prepared to sacrifice heavily in order to assert their freedom from secular institutions of power.

INDEX

Adam:
  creation of, 7-8
  and Eve, 24
Adler, Felix, 79, 82, 95-96, 104
Adventures of Ideas, The (Whitehead),
    134
Aggression, military, 22-23
Agnostics, as religious, 79
Akiba, Rabbi, 8, 26
Altruism:
  drive to, 16
  meaning of, 129-130
Amsterdam Assembly, World Council of
    Churches, 60
Anthropology, culture patterns from, 30,
    43-44, 110
Aquinas, St. Thomas, 37, 108, 120
Aristotle, 111, 118, 121, 124, 126, 129
Artificial insemination, 73
Atomic bomb, *see* Nuclear war
Authority:
  in Protestantism, 4, 55, 56, 58, 70
  in Roman Catholicism, 31, 35-36, 38,
    51, 147

Bacon, Francis, 121
Bailey, Derrick Sherwin, 71-72
Beach, Waldo, 59-60
Behavior, compulsive, 87
  human, 122-124, 135-138, 142-143
Behavioral sciences, 5, 30, 158-159
Bentham, Jeremy, 129
Bible:
  on family ethics, 47, 49, 68-69, 73
  Hebrew, *see* Torah
  and man's relation to God, 34, 55
  moral teaching from, 35

Birth control:
  Ethical Culture views on, 94-95
  and Judaism, 23-25
  Protestant ethics of, 68, 71-73
  Rationalist views of, 132
  and Roman Catholicism, 36, 50-51, 98
Boston University, 145
Brunner, Emil, 72
Bryson, Lyman, 107-144

Calvin, John, 55
Capital punishment, 12, 90-91
Casuistry, lack of, in Protestantism, 4-5,
    70, 148
Catholic, *see* Roman Catholicism
Celibacy:
  in Judaism, 23
  Protestant attitude toward, 71, 72-73
  in Roman Catholicism, 49-50, 72
Children:
  education of, 67-68, 96-101
  as purpose of marriage, 48, 49, 50-51,
    71-72, 93-94
  treatment of, 89-90, 139-142
Christ, *see* Jesus Christ
Christian Socialist Movement, 60
Christianity:
  ethical tradition of, 7
  in history, 125
  and the infinite universe, 79
  love in, 130
  as necessary, 67
  and social action, 59-60
Church:
  as institution, 96-97, 109, 159-160
  in Protestantism, 55, 56, 58, 59
  Roman Catholic, *see* Roman Catholic
    Church
  task of the, 148-149

161